SUNDAY NIGHTS

also by J. RONALD KNOTT

AN ENCOURAGING WORD
Renewed Hearts, Renewed Church
The Crossroads Publishing Co.   1995

ONE HEART AT A TIME
Renewing the Church in the New Millennium
Sophronismos Press   1999

Copies may be ordered from:
Sophronismos Press
939 Eastern Parkway
Louisville, KY 40217

SUNDAY NIGHTS

ENCOURAGING WORDS FOR YOUNG ADULTS

J. RONALD KNOTT

SOPHRONISMOS PRESS   LOUISVILLE, KENTUCKY

SUNDAY NIGHTS

Cover Design: J. Ronald Knott
Book Layout & Design: Becky Jo Hollingsworth

First Printing: September 2000
ISBN: 0-9668969-1-2 (pbk)
Library of Congress Control Number: 00-92838

Cover Photography
Copyright © 2000 by
Morris Press

Printed in the United States by
Morris Publishing
3212 E. Hwy 30
Kearney, NE 68847
1-800-650-7888

To

A.C.T.

ADULT CATHOLICS TOGETHER

Table of Contents

CALLED TO FIDELITY

PREFACE

✠ ▩ ✠ ▩ ✠ ▩

I have always enjoyed being around young adults as a priest. I especially enjoy those Catholic young adults who are still active in the Church. Unlike some of their peers who, at least for now, have thrown out the baby with the bath water, they have been tenacious in trying to internalize their religious upbringing. No longer resisting that religious upbringing, they have begun the challenging process of making the faith of their parents their own personal faith. I find them deeply spiritual, often ravenously so. They want to know God, love God, and serve God; and to feel valued and appreciated by the Church.

One of the many choices facing young adults in every age is whether to embrace or discard all or part of their religious upbringing. Most of them, especially during the turmoil of adolescence, go through some degree of rebellion. Some do not make it through that period of sorting and sifting, but many do make it, and begin their own personal faith journeys. To borrow some words from Shakespeare, they "unthread the rude eye of rebellion and welcome home again discarded faith." It is to this group that I have especially addressed this collection of homilies, almost all of them delivered in St. Robert Bellarmine Chapel over the last year.

I want to offer a special thanks to Dr. Joseph J. McGowen, President of Bellarmine University, who invited me to be its campus priest in the Fall of 1999. His invitation has provided me with an opportunity to accompany many fine young adults, students of Bellarmine University as well as young adults from around the diocese, in their personal faith journeys. It is to these young adults, especially that group of young adults who formed a support group while I was pastor of the Cathedral of the Assumption, that I dedicate this collection of homilies. These young adult Catholics call themselves ACT (Adult Catholics Together). We are happy to welcome them to worship with us at Bellarmine on the first Sunday of each month. ACT has been the model for many young adult groups that emulated them in parishes around the Archdiocese of Louisville, and these groups, too, often join us in St. Robert's Chapel.

I wish to thank my partners in ministry at Bellarmine University: Dr. Fred Rhodes, Dean of Students; Mrs. Melanie-Préjean Sullivan, Campus Minister; and Dr. A.T. Simpson, Professor in the School of Music. They have been most encouraging and helpful.

I appreciate the help of Sister Norma J. Fultz, O.S.B., who graciously agreed to proofread the final manuscript. Finally, I wish to thank Ms. Becky Hollingsworth who has worked tirelessly editing these manuscripts for publication, as well as those of my first two collections of homilies, *An Encouraging Word* and *One Heart At A Time*. To say that I could not have done this without her is, indeed, an understatement.

Father Ron Knott
August, 2000

CALLED TO
FAITH

FAITH

*Blessed are those who have **not** seen and have believed.*
John 20

I have been presiding at Mass here at Bellarmine since the first of September, 1999. I have been amazed by the number of you young adults who make the decision to come to Mass each week. I know that the temptation to do a whole lot of other things on a Sunday night is strong. I know that our culture does not make it easy to maintain a living faith. I also know that our church is not perfect and that it takes great faith to stay in it sometimes. You may not feel all that special, but because you are here, I consider you special. Some of you have a very strong faith. Others are a little shaky in their faith. A few may think they have only a very small grain of faith. No matter! You are here! Jesus said, "With faith the size of a mustard seed, you can move mountains."

When I read the words of today's gospel, I thought of all of you. It's about faith. It is about the faith of those who had the privilege to met Jesus face to face. But it's also about those of us who have believed over the years without actually seeing the one in whom we believe! The apostle, Thomas, was not a silly little bundle of emotions who fell for every belief that came down the pike! No, he wanted proof!

He didn't want hearsay. He didn't want a secondhand

1

Jesus. Thomas wanted to touch the nail holes in Jesus' hands. He wanted to stick his finger into the gapping wound in Jesus' side. Thomas believed only after he had seen and touched and heard. Jesus accepts Thomas' faith, as limited as it was. He did not condemn it. He did not put it down! He granted his wish. Thomas believed! Then, as if Jesus looks out of the storyat us, he speaks directly to us across the centuries, "Blessed are those who have not seen and have believed."

People often speak of faith as accepting the truth of some church teaching, but faith is more than merely believing something is true. Others talk about faith as a thing, something you have one day and lose on another. In English, the word "faith" is used as a noun, but in many languages the word "faith" is a verb, illustrating that faith is not a thing one can own, but an activity that one does! In our gospel reading today, Jesus asks us to do some "faithing!" To "faith" then, means to trust — to trust Jesus enough that we are willing to bet our lives on him; to trust Jesus enough to base our decisions, behaviors, and ways of relating on him. That is a lot more radical than simply believing that something is true. We can believe Jesus existed, preached, died and rose a long time ago, just as the Bible says, but "to faith in Jesus" means that we trust Jesus to direct our lives right here and right now! There is a world of difference between having beliefs about Jesus and trusting Jesus with the direction of our lives, right now, in this world!

Here is an example. You can believe that a swinging bridge will support you. You can even write a paper telling about your belief in the reliability of swinging bridges. You can have engineers inspect the bridge and declare it safe. You can stand at the entrance to the bridge telling curious onlookers that you believe the bridge to be safe. But all you have done is to show that you believe in the safety of the swinging bridge. It is not until you step out onto the bridge that you "faith" that the bridge will hold you up. It is not the talking or the believing, but the risking that is "faithing."

This is what Jesus asks of us. You can believe that Jesus existed. You can quote theologians about the existence of Jesus. You can tell others that you believe that Jesus existed. But it is not until you step out and trust Jesus with your life that you "faith" in Jesus. It is not the talking or the believing, but the risking and trusting that is "faithing." To "faith" in Jesus, to trust Jesus with your life, you must know Jesus. You must have an on-going relationship with Jesus, not just know some facts about him and his life. Unfortunately, there are many in the church who try to get by simply by believing a few facts about Jesus. Sorry! That doesn't work! Before you can **trust** Jesus, you must **know** Jesus, not just a few facts **about** Jesus, or else you may be one of those people who have many beliefs and yet no faith whatsoever!

OK, so we are not there yet! Our ability to "faith" may still be the size of a mustard seed. Like Thomas, Jesus accepts us where we are and calls us to an ever-deepening faith over a life-time. He invites us to "feed on" the Holy Word that we have just heard and to "feed on" his Body and Blood in the Eucharist we are about to share, so that our faith may become stronger and stronger each week. Even on those days when we find "faithing" nearly impossible, we can always be faithful. We can keep gathering together around this pulpit and that altar each week, praying, "Lord, I believe! Help my unbelief!" We are works in progress and that is OK!

OPENNESS

May it be done to me according to your word.

Luke 1

I have been an intentional spiritual seeker since about 1965. It was then that I decided to take charge of my own spiritual growth. I have tried to be deliberate about growing as a person. I have found one basic spiritual principle to be especially helpful. It goes something like this: never underestimate the value of a good disaster! I have learned that with the right attitude toward a seeming disaster, in time those so-called disasters open into amazing blessings. They are often no more than invitations to change and grow. We commit personal and spiritual suicide when we get in the habit of saying "no" to the invitations to grow which are hidden in a so-called disaster.

Let me give you an example of how this spiritual principle works. When I was ordained in 1970, I had my heart set on being an associate pastor at one of the big suburban parishes here in Louisville. I had grown up in the country and I was looking forward to being out of seminary and finally free to take advantage of all that the "big city" had to offer. Two weeks after I was ordained, I got a call from the priest personnel board telling me where I was going to be assigned. They told me that I was being sent to the home missions, down in south central Kentucky, to a seven county

5

cluster of small Catholic mission churches. I thought I would die, right there with the phone in my hand! I begged and pleaded, to no avail. I also knew that the pastor there was known as one of the meanest old priests, especially to young associate pastors! I knew that I was screwed! Their minds were made up and I couldn't exactly quit the priesthood after just two weeks! After all, it had taken me twelve long years of seminary to get there. Angrily, I packed my car, bought a road map and headed south, bitching and moaning to God every mile of the way. I resonated with the famous words of St. Theresa. She supposedly said, after a disastrous day, "Listen God, if this is the way you treat your friends, no wonder you don't have many!" About half way to my first assignment, I had a major conversion experience. I changed my mind. I decided, like Mary, to say to God "let it be" and "bring it on." I knew that I was going to be there for ten years, one way or another, so I decided to change my mind and to go into it with an open mind and to see what might happen. It turned out to be an incredibly wonderful ten years! Because of saying "yes" to God then, I was showered with blessings and opportunities that I could not have imagined!

Mary, the mother of Jesus, was confronted with one of those invitations, only it took a zillion times more courage to say "yes" to the invitation Mary received! A messenger from God delivered the invitation. Mary was a little hesitant. She smelled a rat. She knew that she was in for it, if she said "yes." She was terrified by the prospects of what was being asked of her. But being a woman of God, a God whom she trusted, she made a leap of faith, saying "yes," "let it be," "bring it on!"

Only one woman could be the mother of Jesus, but all of us can have her spiritual courage and say "yes" to God's invitations to us to open up to what God wants to give us. My friends, personal and spiritual suicide is the habit of saying "no" to opportunities to grow and change. Over the years, I have tried to remember this spiritual principle, keeping my eyes open for those periodic invitations to leave the comfort zone that lead to growth and change which God continually presents to me! Another life-changing invitation to take a major step in my personal and spiritual growth came in 1982. I was then pastor of a small country parish outside Lebanon, Kentucky. The people were fabulous. I liked them and they liked me. It was a piece of cake. Comfortable, I expected to stay there for a full twelve year term. Two and a half years into that assignment, about the time things were getting really good, the Archbishop tossed a bomb into my world. He said, "I want you to come to Louisville, to be the cathedral pastor and to see what you can do with it!" He gave me a week to think about it. Like Mary, the invitation scared me. I smelled a rat. I knew that the Cathedral parish was about dead, the buildings were in need of major repair and that there was very little in the bank. I was comfortable in my little country parish. I was attached to it. I battled it back and forth in my mind, deciding initially that I would say, "No, thank you. I don't need the headache. I like it just fine where I'm at!" But in the end I knew that I had to go with it. I knew in my heart of hearts that I had to say "let it be" and "bring it on!" Thank God I did! It turned out to be the most exciting fourteen years of my life. Because I said "yes" to God then, I was showered with blessings and opportunities that I could never have imagined throughout my years at that parish.

I also have a tragic story of a family who said "no" to the invitation to grow and change. It happened when I was down in the southern part of the state. There was a very old couple who had a blind daughter. Because she was blind, they were able to adopt her when they were much older than most adopting couples. In a certain sense, they literally loved her to death. They protected her so much because of her blindness that they had ended up crippling her even more by making her totally dependent on them. She had never been trained to do anything for herself. She always talked about going to the School for the Blind up here in Louisville, but her parents would not hear of it. Because they were getting up in age and the daughter was so dependent, a social worker and I talked her parents into letting her come up here to the School For the Blind so that she could take care of herself should something happen to her aged parents. We finally got her into the school. She loved it, really loved it! But within a few weeks, the blind girl quit the school and returned home to her elderly parents. It seems that the grieving parents had called her and asked her to come home because they were "lonely for her." Personal and spiritual suicide is the result of saying "no" to opportunities to grow and change. That family had that invitation, and they said "no." It was too scary. They loved her to death. By being selfish, they crippled her even more!

My friends, Mary has a lot to teach us tonight. Like her, we all get invitations from God to move into the unknown.

It's OK to be afraid, but it's not OK to give into our fear! God will give us the courage to say "yes," if we ask for it. For me, these invitations have been sort of like God zooming up to me on a big menacing Harley and saying, "Get on! We're going for a ride!" I used to stand there giving myself all the good reasons to say "no." "It's too dangerous. I might get hurt. I'm too scared." Thank God, like Mary, I've had the courage to say, once in a while at least, "OK! Let it be! Bring it on!" Every time I have consciously done that, I have been blessed abundantly.

All of you have had similar invitations from God. Some of you have said "yes," in face of disasters, set-backs, and unwanted outcomes. You know what I am talking about. You know that often what appeared to be a disastrous situation actually turned out to be the occasion of unimagined blessings. You know the truth of "nothing ventured, nothing gained." The spiritual life is about developing your ability to recognize these invitations in life, as well as developing the intestinal fortitude to answer "yes" to them. To all the young adults here, I say, "watch out!" God is especially active in extending these invitations at this point in your life. I pray that you will have the wisdom to recognize your invitations, and the courage to see where they lead.

BLINDNESS

Some of the Pharisees . . . said to him, "Surely we are not also blind, are we?"

John 9

I had to get glasses when I was forty-five years old. I probably needed them for a year or two before that, but I was in denial! I was blaming it on "today's cheap light bulbs" and "the smaller print that printers are using these days." I didn't realize just how much I needed "corrective lenses," as they say in the business, until the summer I went to Greece to celebrate my twenty-fifth anniversary. On the way over I took my glasses off, put them on my lap, fell asleep, and proceeded to wallow on them for the next two and a half hours! When I woke up, I discovered that I was sitting on them! The glasses looked like they had been through a trash compactor. My traveling partner, Father Stoltz, had to lead me around Athens by the hand while we tried to find an optical repair shop. Believe it or not, the same man who helped us find an optical shop also tried to fix us up with a couple of prostitutes. I couldn't even tell what she looked like! Anyway, it took two days to get my glasses back. In the meantime, I was saying a lot of stupid things like, "Yeah, that's beautiful, but what is it?" I had to ask Father Stoltz to read me the menus several times before I could even order a meal. I combed my hair by Braille. Thank God I had a full beard back then so I didn't have to shave. I probably would have slit my own throat. I have a travel tip for you — take two pairs of glasses and save yourself a lot of grief!

I remember another occasion when I could not see, even with my eyes wide open. I was taking a conflict management class. We had to role play an actual conflict situation we had experienced in our ministry. I had a co-worker with whom I could not get along no matter how hard I tried! When we finished the role play the whole class started laughing. They could see something that I could not see. The teacher kept asking me what I observed; I kept coming up with even more ideas to try. The class members laughed again, and I came up with two or three more things I could try to improve the situation. Finally, the instructor stopped, made me look right at him and said, "Ron quit trying! She has told you a hundred times she doesn't want to work with you. When will you take 'no' for an answer? Say 'thank you' and 'good-bye' and move on!" It was a real eye-opener. I had pretty good eyesight at the time. I had no idea that I had such poor insight.

I remember one time when I tried not to see. In October of 1982 I was pastor of a small country parish in Marion County. It was a piece of cake. I loved the people there. They loved me. There wasn't much to do. In fact, that was the hardest part of the job — it was too easy. One day I was in Louisville for a priests' meeting. Archbishop Kelly came up to me and asked, "Would you consider coming to Louisville? I want to "do something" with the Cathedral. It ruined my day. I was happy where I was. I still had almost seven years to go to finish my term as pastor. I kept thinking, "Why would anyone in their right mind want to trade this for a rundown old church in downtown Louisville with no people and no money and lots of expectations?" I almost said "no" on the spot. I didn't want to look at it. I didn't want to think about it. I didn't want to see. I was tempted to go blind on purpose because I didn't want my serene, unchallenged life to be upset!

All three of these "blindnesses" are at work in today's gospel. (1) There is the man born physically blind and spiritually blind. Jesus approaches him, anoints his eyes with a mixture of mud and saliva, and tells him to wash in the pool of Siloam. The man does so and comes back with his sight restored. Coming to full faith and enlightenment, however, goes through stages for the man whom Jesus healed. When he is first questioned by the onlookers, he knows only that "the man they call Jesus" healed him. When brought before the Pharisees, he advances to calling Jesus "a prophet." When they persist in their questioning, he calls Jesus "a man from God." Finally, when he is expelled from the synagogue, Jesus asks him outright, "Do you believe in the Son of Man?" He answers, "I do believe!" It is only after this series of testings that the healed man comes to **full** faith and insight into the person of Jesus. (2) Then there are the religious authorities who could see physically but who had gradually become spiritually blind. They were thoroughly convinced that they already knew all that needed to be known. Years of smug certitude had made their minds hard and impenetrable. Their certitude made them blind to God's activity even when it took place in front of them. (3) Finally, there were the blind man's parents who knew the truth about their son, but deliberately chose to go deaf, dumb, and blind, selfishly refusing to say anything about the matter, lest they lose their place in the synagogue and have their comfortable lives upset. "We don't know anything about this! He is of age; he can speak for himself. Ask him!"

In the final analysis, we are presented with people who couldn't see and people who wouldn't see. Physical blindness is a serious loss, but it's not the most tragic kind of blindness. When I was at a Cathedral, we had two blind members of the parish. They seemed to do quite well. They didn't want sympathy. They just needed the world to remove more of its obstacles. Many of us, on the other hand, have a spiritual blindness, whereby we gradually lose our vision because we choose not to see. This disease is reversible, if caught in time. If healing is to begin, there is a lot of denial going on that must be pierced. As the old saying goes, "There is none so blind as him who will not see."

One of our major blind spots centers around the concept of "living well." For most of us, "living well" means living comfortably — a nice house, nice vacations, nice clothes and nice food. For a smaller number of us, "living well" means living correctly — being honest, generous, spiritual, loyal and engaged in making the world a better place. For some "living well" means owning goods. For others, "living well" means being good. Some people build their lives on "having goods" with little regard for ethical considerations. Some people build their lives on "being good" without having much joy in their lives. On the surface, "living well" and "being good" seem contradictory. They are not. Blindness involves the failure to balance the two — living pleasantly and living ethically. Because we fail to see this need for balance, the "be good" people are now on a major crusade against the "feel good" people. They will probably drag us off the other side of the road and , left unchecked, could turn this country into a Christian version of Ayatollah Kohmeni's Iran.

Religious terrorism is rampant in other parts of the world. What makes us think it would not be possible here? Like the Pharisees in this gospel story, religious fanatics are convinced that they can see clearly when, in fact, they too are blind. Heresy, I have always heard, is the truth exaggerated to the point of distortion. The truth of the matter is that we cannot live pleasantly very long without living ethically. Ask any of the dead civilizations! On the other hand, I still have hope that our country will not choose to be seduced by the simplistic slogans of zealotry. Zealotry always fails because it tries to demonstrate its commitment by forcing commitment on others. Zealots like to stage self-congratulatory productions of smug superiority. We do well to ignore zealots on both ends of the spectrum and listen to the less shrill voices of reason and hope. "Living well" is about balancing our need to live comfortably with our need to live correctly. If we are not healed of this blindness, on the left and on the right, we're going to be in a heap of trouble very, very soon!

CATHOLIC

In truth, I see that God shows no partiality. Rather, in every nation whoever fears him and acts uprightly is acceptable to him.

Acts 10

Shortly after I was ordained, I attended a reception. I dressed up in my new black suit and Roman collar. I had not yet learned just how risky that can be! Sometimes it's like wearing a big red circle painted on your chest as a target for the slings and arrows of anyone who has a beef against the Catholic Church. The gripe might be about something that happened in the sixteenth century, something that happened when they were in the second grade, or something that happened last week in a parish on the other side of town. As I was charming my way through the room, I was suddenly confronted by an angry young woman. She yelled loud enough for everyone to hear, "I can't believe that any intelligent person these days would choose to be a priest, much less a Catholic! I got out of that silliness a long time ago!" My face turned beet red. I was stunned and embarrassed. I had worked hard for twelve long years and overcome many obstacles to be able to wear that collar. I was proud of it, and it felt as if she had spit on it in front of everyone!

That encounter turned out to be just the beginning. Something similar happened several more times over the years. One particular event stands out in my memory. In my early years as a priest, I was assigned to the home missions of our diocese to start a mission parish and to be the first Catholic priest to live in that county. Not too long after I arrived, I decided to go to the county ministerial association meeting. I put on my black suit and Roman collar and walked into a room full of fellow pastors. When the host minister saw me, he abruptly stood up and walked out. After a few minutes, his secretary came in with a message which read, "I can no longer be part of this group, now that it has a Catholic priest in it! Would you please leave my church!" Again my face turned beet red. I was stunned and embarrassed. In a few minutes, the rest of us got up, walked out, and went to another church across the street.

Looking back, I see that these experiences actually helped me. They made me think. They made me ask myself just why I am a Catholic and not a member of some easy, less complicated, church. I have studied, experienced, and worked in the Catholic Church up close and personal as a priest for thirty years now. I have concluded that I like being Catholic. In fact, I wouldn't switch for anything. Oh, yes, I know that many of the criticisms hurled at the Catholic Church are true. We are a little old-fashioned. Some of us, sometimes, have been insensitive, maybe even cruel. We have taken our eye off the prize several times in our long history. But when it's all said and done, what's good about the Catholic Church makes up for all that's bad about it! After all these years, I find myself consciously Christian, deliberately Catholic, and unapologetically ecumenical.

What does it mean to be "catholic?" The word "catholic" means "universal" and "inclusive." The words of Saint Peter in our first reading today put it this way, "In truth, I see that God shows no partiality. Rather, in every nation whoever fears him and acts uprightly is acceptable to him." It took a while for Peter to get to this view. It went against every bone in his body. He had been taught from childhood that God hated Gentiles, but in a vision God revealed to him that, far from rejecting those who were not Jewish, God welcomed them as followers of Jesus, together with the original Jewish disciples. We are told that even those who accompanied Peter were astounded that the gift of the Holy Spirit was being poured out on Gentiles, as well as Jews. Little by little this "catholic" view was adopted by the whole church and officially ratified at the Council of Jerusalem by the body of apostles.

After 2,000 years, our church is still "catholic," still "inclusive," still teaching that God "shows no partiality. In every nation whoever fears God and acts uprightly is acceptable to him." The Second Vatican Council teaches us that even though the Catholic Church has been endowed with all divinely revealed truth, "the Catholic Church rejects nothing which is true and holy in other religions. She looks with sincere respect upon those ways of conduct and of life, those rules and teachings which, though differing in many particulars from what she holds and sets forth, nevertheless often reflect a ray of that Truth which enlightens all men." It calls Protestants our "brothers and sisters from whom we can learn much." It recalls our special connection to the Jewish people. It says that the church "looks with esteem on the Moslems." It speaks with respect for Hindus and Buddhists. It teaches us that "the Church rejects, as foreign to the mind of Christ, any discrimination against men or harassment of them because of their race, color, condition of life or religion." It further admits that even though the church teaches and believes all this, we have sometimes "failed to live by these teachings with all the fervor we should."

We are not a national church, we are a "catholic" church. We are universal. No one has demonstrated this better than Pope John Paul II, the most recent successor of Peter. He has traveled to most of the countries of the world. He speaks many, many languages. He chooses bishops and cardinals from every culture on the planet. He has celebrated Mass for young people, sick people, poor people, and people of every color and culture. He has visited mosques and temples, prayed with Protestants, Moslems and Jews, and canonized saints of every country on earth. The Pope before him was Italian. He is a son of Poland. The next could be African!

Among the priests and seminarians of Louisville, we have African Americans, Vietnamese, and Hispanics. All this makes me proud to be called "catholic." We are not perfect, we have a long way to go yet, but we are universal and inclusive.

Vatican Council II also notes that "there can be no ecumenism worthy of the name without a change of heart." To be truly "catholic," one has to keep an open mind and an open heart. We have to resist the natural human tendency to separate, exclude, marginalize, and condemn people who are different. We see the ugly face of racism, sexism, ageism and religious intolerance every night on the news. Like Peter, we need a change of heart before we can say, "In truth, I see that God shows no partiality. Rather, in every nation whoever fears him and acts uprightly is acceptable to him." To be truly "catholic," we have to see the world with God's eyes, the eyes of love and compassion!

CALLED TO
DISCIPLESHIP

CALLED

". . . if you are called, reply, "Speak, Lord, for your servant is listening."

I Samuel 3

☒ ✠ ☒ ✠ ☒ ✠ ☒

I've been a priest for thirty years. Most of that time I was pastor of a parish. I had a parish in the home mission area of our diocese. I had a parish in the country. I had a parish in downtown Louisville. When old acquaintances ask me what I am doing these days, I tell them that I am the Archdiocesan Vocation Director. What does a Vocation Director do? He does what the old priest, Eli, does in today's first reading; he helps people hear their calls and challenges them to answer! Instead of being the pastor of a particular parish, I go from parish to parish every Sunday telling people, especially young adults, that God is calling them to something and that they need to pay attention and respond. I talk a little about the call to priesthood and religious life and invite anyone who wonders if they are being called to this way of life to contact me so that we can explore that call together. For those who are interested in priesthood, I help them get into the seminary and oversee their training. Even though that is a full time job, I enthusiastically accepted the invitation to preside at liturgy and preach here at Bellarmine every weekend. Like Eli in our first reading, I am hoping that I can be of help to some of you as I remind you from this pulpit that you are being called to something and as I challenge you to listen and respond.

Today we have a beautiful story about being called, discerning a call and answering a call. In the text just before our story begins, it says that this event took place during a time like our own, when people were not paying all that much attention to God. Samuel, we are told, was himself not familiar with the Lord. In fact, he was so unfamiliar with the Lord that he did not even recognize God's voice. He mistook it for that of the old priest, Eli. Again, Samuel is so unfamiliar with the Lord that he has to be called three times! It is Eli, who is familiar with the Lord, who encourages Samuel to reply if he hears the call again. After Samuel responds to the one who is calling him, he is graced, he is given all that he needs to excel as an effective preacher and prophet. "Samuel grew up, and the Lord was with him, not permitting any word of his to be without effect."

This story about being called, discerning a call, and answering a call is directed, not just to some of us, but to all of us. God has created each and every one of us to do him some definite service. God has committed some work to us which he has not committed to anyone else. We have a mission. We each have a call. We may be deaf to it, run from it, deny it, or refuse to do it, but won't be really happy until we know what it is and do it!

When they consider what they should do in life, many people today do not know about, much less think about, what God may be calling them to be. No one sits down with them and tells them that they have a vocation, a God-given call, one for which they must listen in their heart of hearts. Our frenetic lifestyle is not conducive to the kind of intense listening that is required. Pleasing parents or doing what others expect may even take the place of searching one's heart. Some may spend years following a path outlined for them by others before they stop to think and feel and search their own hearts. Many young people are taught to choose careers that will bring in the most money, whether they really like the work or not, believing that if they have plenty of money, they can buy the things that will make them happy. There is nothing wrong with money, but surely most of us know that the simple pursuit of money alone will not bring happiness. The pursuit of your God-given call, on the other hand, will make you happy and may even bring you money. (One of my favorite books is entitled *Do What You Love And The Money Will Follow*.) In our story today, when Samuel responds to the one who is calling him, God blesses him and graces him throughout his life, as he becomes increasingly effective in what he does! The same will be true for you: if you hear God's call and answer God's call, God will bless and grace you all the days of your life. With or without money, you will be happy!

Your purpose in this world is to serve God in some way. You may be called to help thousands, even millions. You may be called to help just one person in an intense way. You may be called to marriage and raising children. You may be called to teach, heal, invent, create art, run for office or entertain. You may be called to preach, spend your life in prayer for others or give your life in full time ministry for the good of God's people. Whatever your call, your purpose in this world is to serve God in some way. You will not be truly happy until you find out what it is and respond to it with courage, enthusiasm, and faith!

The church needs good marriages, good parents, good doctors, good teachers, and good politicians. The church needs good nuns, religious brothers, and deacons. The church needs faithful single people. But the church especially needs priests at this time. The Catholic population is growing, while the numbers of priests to serve that growing population is shrinking. Sometimes, one or more parishes have to share one priest. Sometimes the bishop has to close little churches altogether, especially when they are close to a big one! All this is hard on Catholic people, who need the attention of their priests, just as it is hard on priests who are often stretched to the breaking point.

All of us have a vocation. I was called to be a priest. I love it more every year. I believe that if young men heard from more of us happy priests (and most of us are happy) they might be more willing to listen to God to see if they are being called to serve him as a priest. My job is to go around the diocese challenging people to listen to God with their hearts to see what God wants them to do with their lives. I want to ask young women and men to listen to God to see if they are being called to be full-time lay ministers, religious sisters, and religious brothers. I especially want to ask young men to listen to God to see if they are being called to be priests.

And so, I am here today to remind all of you, especially the young adults here, that you have a call. Listen to your heart of hearts. Ask God to give you insight and courage.

When you hear your call, respond with courage and pursue your call with passion, as the young Samuel did in today's first reading. Remember, it is not the easy things that bring the greatest happiness. The church needs priests. If you are not called, talk it up to those you think might make good priests. Plant seeds in the minds of young people. Pray for more priests. Pray for the priests we have! And if there is anyone here who has ever toyed with the idea of being a priest, call me and we will talk!

BAPTIZED

. . . Jesus came from Nazareth . . . and was baptized . . .
Mark 1

I was baptized by my grandmother! That's right, my grandmother! I discovered that fact a few years back, by accident, when I got the bright idea to start celebrating my entry into the church, my adoption into the family of God, as well as my actual birthday. I assumed that I had been taken to church a week or two after I was born. That was the practice back then. I called the priest at my home parish down in Meade County, holding the phone as he looked my name up in the church baptismal book. When he came back on the phone, he told me that I had been baptized by my grandmother on the same day I was born! I never knew that! I did know that I was born at home. I did know that both my mother and I almost died in the birthing process. I did know that my grandmother was a country midwife and had helped my mother during the delivery, but no one had told me that my grandmother had baptized me because I was in immediate danger of dying. She knew what I would later learn: in case of a life-threatening emergency, anyone can perform a baptism.

Jesus was baptized in today's gospel. You were baptized too! Do know when you were baptized, by whom, why and how? Have you ever really thought about your own baptism and about what it means? Unfortunately, many people in the church haven't! The church has been working pretty hard for the last thirty years to change that! It may take another thirty years to really change people's awareness of just how important the sacrament of baptism really is!

We may not have thought much about our own baptisms, but we should have! We have had plenty of things to remind us of it on a regular basis. (1) We have always had the practice of dipping our hands into holy water and crossing ourselves as we enter a Catholic Church, but unfortunately people don't always make the connection to baptism. Each time we do that, cross ourselves with holy water, we are reminding ourselves that we are **baptized** people! Through our baptisms, we became adopted children of God and heirs to heaven itself! (2) Most of us who were baptized when we were children were "confirmed" in our baptism when we were teen-agers. In the Sacrament of Confirmation, we took over responsibility for our own spiritual life from our parents and childhood teachers. (3) Every Sunday since our baptisms and confirmations, we have repeated the Creed, that formal summary of our faith. We repeat, every Sunday, that we believe in "one God: Father, Son and Holy Spirit!" It was in that name we were baptized! (4) We sprinkle rings with holy water at weddings. (5) We sprinkle holy water on people when we renew our baptismal commitments together every Easter. (6) We even sprinkle holy water on caskets and dress them up in a white baptismal robe at funerals, all because we want to remind ourselves that we are baptized into the body of Christ, that we are God's children and heaven bound.

Even with all these reminders, the Fathers of Vatican Council II initiated several reforms to remind us even more intentionally of the importance of baptism in the life of the church. (1) The role of godparents has been reduced, while the role of parents as primary teachers of the faith to their children has been restored. (2) Parents must go through required preparation on that role as primary teachers of the faith to their children and show that they practice the faith they profess. (3) Baptisms are now regularly celebrated on Sundays, with the whole assembly present, not in some dark corner of the church on a Sunday afternoon. (4) Adults are now trained extensively, baptized on Easter, and given the option of full immersion in many places. If an adult who seeks membership in our church has already been baptized in a Protestant Church, that baptism is respected and honored: new members are not re-baptized as they enter the Roman Catholic Church. (5) Many new Catholic churches now have large immersion pools in the center aisle as we enter the church to remind us that our first entrance into the church was through baptism! Yes, if you add it all up, there are hundreds of ways the church honors, respects, and gives baptism its place of honor in the life of the church.

One final question: what is the point of baptism? Jesus began his public ministry at his baptism in the Jordan River. At his baptism, Jesus received his divine commission to begin the work that God had sent him into the world to do —

opening all kinds of blind eyes, freeing all types of prisoners, lifting up all forms of oppression and showing people the incredible love God has for every human person.

Having become children of the light, living in a sinful world but rejecting sin and the glamour of evil, you and I were commissioned at our baptisms to carry on that same ministry in the name of Jesus. Unfortunately, we have millions of baptized members in our church who haven't the foggiest understanding of what their baptism means. Many of us still believe that we were baptized into the church so that it can serve us! As members of the church, especially these days, we seem to be long on asserting our rights, but short on accepting our duties. We became members of the church, not to be served **by** the church, but to be of service to others **through** the church. At our baptisms we were made disciples, ambassadors, and personal representatives of Jesus Christ, sent in his name to heal the world. We were initiated into a vast army of baptized persons who have gone out, in Jesus' name, to continue his saving work in the world over the last 2,000 years.

Baptism is a beginning. It marked the beginning of Jesus' ministry 2,000 years ago. It marks the beginning of our commitments to carry on that ministry in every age since. When you come in here every Sunday and dip your hand in this water, re-signing yourself with it, in the name of the Father, Son, and Holy Spirit, you are recalling your baptism. You do it again when we recite the Creed together every Sunday, reminding ourselves that we believe in one God — Father, Son, and Holy Spirit — in whose name we were sealed. And finally, one day, your family will roll you into a church one last time, you will be sprinkled with baptismal water and your casket will be dressed with a white pall similar to your white baptismal dress, reminding us once again that you were an adopted child of God, sent to the world in his name to carry on some part of his work and destined to become an heir to the very kingdom of God Himself!

Maybe some of you will go to the trouble of finding out exactly what day you were baptized, putting it on your calendar each year like you would your birthday, and using it as a time to take a serious spiritual inventory each year. That alone could be the beginning of a whole new spiritual awakening!

GIFTED

He called in his servants and handed his funds over to them according to each one's abilities. To one he disbursed five thousand silver pieces, to a second two thousand, and to a third a thousand.

Matthew 25

I have been a home missionary, country pastor, cathedral rector, and traveling evangelist. Three years ago I became the Vocation Director for the Archdiocese of Louisville. My job now involves traveling among our one hundred twenty-one parishes to remind people, especially young adults, that they have a vocation, a call, to serve God and God's people in some way — as a parent, teacher, lawyer, law officer, doctor, artist, nurse, musician, spouse, inventor, scientist, priest, author, farmer, administrator, or in hundreds of other ways. I challenge people to follow their vocations, to answer their calls, with courage and faith. Every single one of us is called, but not all of us are called to perform the same service. As our second reading puts it, "we have gifts that differ," and "not all members have the same function."

Every one of us here is a unique, one-of-a-kind expression of God's love and creativity. God dreamed us, created us, and minds us. Besides being special and unique, we are sent here for a purpose. We are not here by accident. We are not here just for our own good. We have something to do here that can be done by no one else. If we fail to do it, we not only suffer, but the whole world suffers with us. To be born is to have a mission. Our first responsibility, then, is to find out what our mission is. Only then can we carry it out with all the deliberateness we can muster. How do we discover our mission, our purpose, our call? The answer lies in the depths of our hearts! We can hear and understand our calls only by listening to our heart of hearts. That takes some quality, quiet time with the God who made us!

Our very happiness depends on discovering our calls, our purposes in the world. If we are in rhythm with our calls, our happiness will increase. If we are out of rhythm with our calls, our lives will become painfully out of sync. We will be unhappy without knowing why; we will jump aimlessly from one thing to another, hoping to bump into happiness by accident. As a priest I have met numerous young adults who are still stuck, still paralyzed, still living at home, still living in chronic dull pain, without direction or purpose, well into their forties. My heart aches for them.

A call is not something that comes from God as an order, but rather as an invitation. We have a choice. We can tune out the longings we feel rather than act on them. We sometimes do that because we fear what those longings may demand of us in pursuing them. Like the servant in today's gospel, some choose to bury their talents even from their own eyes because they are afraid — and behind fear is laziness. When we bury our talents, we sabotage our own happiness. Even those who love us — parents, friends and peers

— can sometimes conspire to divide us against ourselves, leading us away from who we are. In the end we must listen to our own hearts and act courageously on our own behalf! In the end, we are responsible for making something out of ourselves from what has been given us. The ultimate cowardice, I believe, is to blame others for our fear and laziness in the face of getting a life, like the servant who buried his talent and then blamed the master who gave it to him. "I failed because I was afraid of you." "It's your fault because you are so demanding."

Following our calls from God, becoming who we are, is a risk. It brings both exhilaration and terror. Like the servants in the parable in whom the master invested, the challenge to grow our talents does not mean automatic success. Mistakes are allowed. Cowardice isn't. God gives us a challenge and calls us is to rise to the occasion. The coward who buried his talents is the one who loses all in the end because he risked nothing and played it safe.

Graduates! God has invested much in you. You are created in God's image and likeness. God calls you to engage life, not back off from it. Your parents have invested much in you. They have worked hard to make sure you go into adulthood with all the tools you need to make something of yourselves. Like the servants in the parable, honor your parents by showing them what you can do with what you have been given! Bellarmine University has invested much in you. You have learned life skills and professional skills that should serve you for the rest of your life. Take these skills and grow them. You have been students. Now become teachers. What you have been given has been given to share. Share what you have learned with the world and help leave it a better place than you found it.

A famous spiritual teacher once said, "The glory of God is a fully alive human being." This is your call! This is your challenge! All of you are talented. Some of you have been given more talents than others. But that is no cause for bragging or smug superiority, because it is of those to whom much is given that much will be required. Whether you have one talent or fifty, take all that has been invested in you and see what you can do with it! And when you are called in at the end of your life is to make an accounting, you can hear God say to you, "Well done, good and faithful servant! Enter into the joy of your master!" The saddest people are not those who tried and failed, but those who never tried at all. The saddest people on earth are those who reach the end of their lives and have never really lived! Remember this parable! Take your talents and gifts, get out there and grab life by the horns, and see what you can do with it! Your happiness depends on it! This is why you are here!

SENT

Go into the whole world and proclaim the gospel to every creature.

Mark 16

As far as I know, Jesus never held a revival, never published a book of sermons, never taught a course on preaching, never conducted a parish mission, never preached around the globe like the Pope, never had a radio or TV ministry. The people who knew him were few, the area he visited was small, the length of time for which he preached was short, yet the "good news" he announced to the world has spread to the ends of the earth. He simply planted it in the hearts of a small band of followers over a three year period and told them to "go into the whole world and proclaim it to every creature." They were successful beyond their wildest imaginations. Because of their preaching, we sit here as Christians 2,000 years later!

Contrary to popular opinion, the task of "proclaiming the gospel to every creature" is not restricted to ordained ministers: bishops, priests and deacons. Vatican Council II reminded us that "every baptized member of the church is a missionary," duty bound to do his or her share in the missionary work among the nations. The work of evangelization is a basic duty of the whole People of God. In other words, it's not an option. We proclaim the gospel, first and foremost, by living a profoundly Christian life, not by banging on doors and preaching at each other. By living a profoundly Christian life, we will be "the light of the world," "the salt of the earth," and "a city built on a hill." After all, it is not those who say, "Lord, Lord," but those who **do** the will of God who are the most effective and believable proclaimers of the gospel. By living a profoundly Christian life, Christians proclaim the gospel, becoming a "kind of leaven in the dough."

There is unity of purpose, but a diversity of service. In other words, we proclaim the gospel in various ways, but we are **all** called to proclaim it! The main duty of lay men and women is to proclaim the gospel by their lives and works in their homes, in their social groups and in their own professional circles. Christian husbands and wives are witnesses of the faith to each other. People marry, not for their own good, but for the good of others, especially their spouses and children. If marriage contributes to personal salvation, it is through service of others that it does so. By living profoundly Christian lives, marriage partners inspire each other to live the Christian life even more deeply. Parents are the first to communicate the faith to their children. By word and example, they train their children in living the Christian life and in carrying on the work of Jesus Christ in today's world. Some do it in heroic ways by caring for elderly parents and through adoption and the parenting of foster children. Besides carrying out their call to proclaim the gospel in marriage and family life, marriage partners do it in the Church and in the world. The laity proclaim the gospel, whether married or single, by engaging in the various apostolic activities of the church: missionary work, teaching, youth ministry, liturgical ministry, parish administration, political service, national and international social justice work and a whole host of other apostolic activities.

How can the laity proclaim the gospel in their own unique way, unless they believe? How can they believe unless they have heard? How can they hear unless someone is sent? Priesthood, like marriage, is directed toward the salvation of others. Priests exist to build up the People of God. Priests build up the People of God mainly by preaching the gospel. Preaching during the celebration of the Sacraments is a priest's **primary** task. Through the Word of God, the spark of faith is struck in the hearts of unbelievers and nourished in the hearts of believers.

Yesterday, we ordained six new priests for the Archdiocese of Louisville. As the archdiocesan Vocation Director, it was my job and privilege to oversee their training. If priests have as their primary duty the proclamation of the gospel through preaching, then preaching must be at the very top of the list of the many, many things they will be called to do in the months and years ahead. Good preaching will not automatically fall from their lips simply because they have been ordained. They must be vigilant and fight to keep preaching at the top of their list. If their preaching is to draw unbelievers to the faith and nourish the faith of believers, there are several things they must do. I have identified four. These four points apply not just to those of us who are called to preach, but to all the baptized who are called to proclaim the gospel in various other ways, as spouses, parents, teachers, and lay ministers of every type.

(1) We priests are called to preach the gospel, the "good news" of Jesus Christ. .We must first of all know what the "good news" is! That might sound obvious, but it isn't. In my thirty years of preaching and, in the last few years, of teaching people how to preach, I have discovered that there are probably millions of Christians who have sat in church their whole lives and still have never clearly and concisely heard the "good news" preached to them. Why? Because there are preachers who cannot tell you in a nutshell what the "good news" is! The "good news" is this — God loves every human being on this planet without condition: no ands, ifs, or buts about it. Our job as preachers is to announce this fact to as many people as possible, in as many ways as possible, using as many examples as possible, as often as possible, wherever possible.

(2) The Word of God must be alive in our own hearts. *Nemo dat quod non habet.* "You can't give it if you don't have it." If the gospel is to be a living Word, not just a speech about Biblical facts, we must be hearers of the Word ourselves. We must know, love, and listen to God. We must know, love, and listen to ourselves. We must know, love, and listen to the Scriptures. We must know, love, and listen to the people to whom we preach. As the bishop instructs deacons at ordination when he hands the Scriptures to them, "Believe what you read, teach what you believe, and practice what you teach." God's Word must burn in our hearts. If the Word of God burns in our hearts, we will be driven to

communicate it. As William Faulkner put it, "If the story is in you, it has to come out!" To have a burning passion for sharing the Word of God, we must have an energetic spiritual life. As our Baptist brothers and sisters remind us, we must have a personal relationship with Jesus Christ.

(3) We must know what preaching is and what it isn't. A priest is a medium between God and people. As a preacher, our job is to apply the truth of the gospel to the concrete circumstances of life. We are the people called to translate the words of scripture into words people today can understand. We must have insight and be articulate. When we preach, people must be able to say, "Aha! Now I get it!" The pulpit is not given to us as a platform to impress people with how much we learned in seminary. It is not a stage given to us to entertain people like a stand-up comedian, nor to rant and rave about our pet peeves, nor to pass judgment on the weak, nor to do parish business, nor to sell the latest diocesan program. Preaching is not about the preacher. We are messengers, not the message. We are simply earthenware jars that hold a great treasure. We must never let the crock become more important than the treasure.

(4) We must respect those to whom we are sent to preach. We are not above you. We are not your judges. Our words should "bring **glad** tiding to the poor, liberty to captives, sight to the blind and release to prisoners." When we must challenge people, we need to speak the truth with love! When people come to our pulpits looking for bread, we must not hand them stones. If we are not prepared, then we should not preach. Better to be honest with people than waste their precious time ad libbing some warmed-over drivel or bor-

ing them with trite pious platitudes.

We are all called to "proclaim the gospel" in some way. In whatever way you are called to do it, do it well! As the Hallmark greeting card company puts it, "care enough to send the very best."

INTRODUCTIONS

They came bringing to him a paralytic carried by four men. Unable to get near Jesus because of the crowd, they opened up the roof above him. After they had broken through, they let down the mat on which the paralytic was lying.

Mark 2

Picture it! Palestine, first century! The town of Capernaum! Jesus had just gotten home after a preaching tour of the local synagogues! News travels fast! Hearing that Jesus is home, a huge crowd gathers outside his front door to hear him preach in his own living room! Hearing that Jesus is home, the orthodoxy police from Jerusalem show up to check his sermon for heresy. Hearing that Jesus is home, four men arrive carrying a paralyzed friend in a blanket. "Excuse us! Excuse us!" No one budges.

Desperate situations call for desperate measures. Where there's a will, there's a way! Unable to get through the door, the four men drag their poor paralyzed friend up on the roof, for God's sake, cutting a hole and lowering him right smack dab in front of Jesus! If the scene were not so poignant, it would be laughable! Jesus must have been impressed by their determination and faith!

There are many things going on in this story. I could talk about the forgiveness and healing that Jesus offered the sick man. I could talk about the argument Jesus had with the religious authorities about his authority to forgive sins. But I was fascinated by the faith and determination of the four men who carried their friend to Jesus. It was their belief in Jesus, their determination to overcome all barriers, not the pleading of the paralyzed man, that moved Jesus to work this miracle. To go to such measures, dragging a poor crippled man up on the roof, tells us that these people were both convinced of the power of Jesus to heal, and dedicated to helping their suffering friend.

Have you ever "brought someone to Jesus?" Do you know anyone who needs the healing power of God's love? Do you believe in the reality of God's love so much, are you so convinced of it that you would be willing to introduce others who need to know of it? By our baptisms, we are all called to be "evangelists," people who bring people to Jesus. I am certainly not suggesting that you go out and buy a big Bible and a megaphone and stand in the cafeteria and preach. In fact, it might be good **not** to do that kind of talking, which might drive more people away from Jesus. There is a place for preaching, but as Jesus put it, "It is not those who **say**, "Lord, Lord," but those who **do** the will of my Father."

People marry, not simply to have their own needs met, but to meet the needs of their partners. Married people, we are taught by the church, marry for the salvation of their partners. They pledge to lead each other to Jesus, not by preaching to each other, but by the way they treat each other. Marriage is meant to make holy those who enter it! Parents, we are taught by the church, have the primary responsibility to lead their children to Jesus. The Catechism of the Catholic Church says "the Christian home is the place where children receive the first proclamation of the faith." Those of you who intend to marry, have, I hope, already gone through the sorting out of adolescence. Maybe you even drifted away from the church for a while. Now is the time you must become students of the faith, by your own free choice, so as to be prepared to share the faith with your spouse and children. *Nemo dat quod non habet*. If you don't have it, you can't give it!

Marriage and family life are wonderful for most people, but the single life can be wonderful too. More and more people have chosen it. There are certain advantages to being single. Single people have more personal freedom and flexibility. They tend to have more time and discretionary money. Freedom, time, and resources in the hands of a single person can be very helpful in bringing people to God. Single, young adults can be very effective in bringing others to Jesus. One way might be to invite your non-practicing Catholic friends to come to Mass with you. Another might be to consider some of the opportunities which grow each year for working full time in the church.

Priests, hopefully, bring people to Jesus! A priest's primary responsibility is preaching. It's an awesome task to stand before a group of people and try to break open the Word in such a way that people are introduced to Jesus in a deeper way. To preach effectively one has to know Jesus, not just a bunch of facts about Jesus! A priest presides at the celebration of the sacraments: he receives members into the church in baptism, he presides at the Eucharist and feeds people with the Body and Blood of Jesus, he announces God's forgiveness in the Sacrament of Reconciliation, he leads the sick of mind and soul to the healing power of Jesus in the Sacrament of Anointing, he witnesses marriage vows and the formation of new families. It is an awesome responsibility. As a priest, one never feels good enough or worthy enough. Thank God, we can depend on God's help.

We are all called to bring each other to Jesus. We are our brothers' and sisters' keepers. It's right there in the very first pages of the Bible. We are God's family. Scripture is clear. God deals with us, not as individuals, but as individual members of a family. The church is a family of believers. We come here, not just to "get Jesus," but also to "give Jesus" to each other. No church can be strong and vibrant and focused if every one of its members is weak, lifeless, and disengaged.

I published a collection of homilies last year entitled *One Heart At A Time*. It was a collection of homilies on how to renew the church in the new millennium. In them I try to make the point that it is useless to keep up our endless search for some kind of magical organizational change that will fix the church. What will fix the church has to happen **within** the hearts of individual believers. If we are ever going to really renew the church, it will be "one heart at a time." In other words, probably the **very best way** to bring others to Jesus is by example, by renewing our own faith!

CENTERED

Jesus stood in their midst and said to them, "Peace be with you."

Luke 24

❖ ✠ ❖ ✠ ❖ ✠ ❖

On May 16th, I will celebrate my thirtieth anniversary as a priest. I can hardly believe it myself! Even though it has not always been easy, I wouldn't trade it for anything! In many ways it has been a lot like a long boat trip down the Colorado River. There have been moments of peace and calm, even bits of tediousness, but for the most part it has been an exciting, challenging, and even scary "shooting of the rapids!" The first half of my seminary training was the calm before the storm. Vatican II happened halfway through my twelve years of seminary. The Catholic Church changed, not with a whimper, but with a bang! One semester we wore long black cassocks to class — the next semester we wore shorts! One semester we could be kicked out for even thinking about drinking a beer at school — the next semester the monastery opened a beer and pizza place on campus! One semester we were not allowed to go home until Christmas — the next semester we could have our own cars and come and go as we pleased! It was that drastic! The changes kept coming and coming and coming, never slowing up for fifteen years, until Pope John Paul II was elected and put on the brakes! Some of us loved the excitement of all that churning and fermenting and changing. Others absolutely hated it. But whether we loved it or hated it, it was one hell of a trip for those of us who went through it!

So when I was ordained in 1970, I knew that I was going to be a priest during one of the most tumultuous periods of church history, and I knew that I needed to anchor myself to something solid or I wouldn't last. With all that turmoil, I knew I could either jump out of the boat or be thrown out of it! There were twelve of us ordained in 1970 and only five of us are left! I knew I could not control what was happening outside me, so I had to control what went on inside me. I had to choose how I would react to all that was going on outside of me! I decided to ask God for a "peaceful center" that "no storm can shake." I decided to find a way to avoid abandoning ship because I could not control the waves and the wind. I decided to ask God to help me "keep on keepin' on" even in a storm. God has given me what I needed, when I needed it, at least for thirty years now!

In the last thirty years, I have certainly needed that "peaceful center." I have been a home missionary, country pastor, cathedral rector, college teacher, seminary professor, author, retreat master, and motivational speaker. I have been threatened by the KKK. I have had a knife pulled on me in church. I have been denounced by radio ministers. I lived alone in near isolation for almost eight years. The cathedral cracked during the renovation and almost fell down while I was pastor. I was stalked by a crazy man for almost eight years. I lost both parents and several friends to death. During each one of those episodes, I always went back to my "peaceful center" that "no storm can shake." From that spot deep in my heart, I somehow found the courage to face all these scary events. It is a place in my heart where God lives and lets me know that everything will be all right.

In the gospel today, Jesus appears to his small band of disoriented, disappointed, scared to death disciples and wishes them "peace." They had given up everything to follow Jesus, and their world had been completely shattered on Good Friday. Their master had been killed. All their hopes had collapsed. They were completely devastated and had no idea where to turn. "Peace be with you! Peace is my gift to you!" With that gift, "a peaceful center that no storm could shake," these disciples got up and faced the world, did marvelous things they never thought possible, took the gospel to the ends of the world, accepted beatings, torture, shipwrecks, and prison. Most ended up facing martyrdom.

Most people think "peace" means the absence of conflict, war, suffering, and problems. They think "peace" is a time when everything is just right. It may be someday, but for now "peace" is possible only from the inside out. Jesus offers each and every one of us "a peaceful center" in the midst of all the storms, setbacks, and problems of life. It is there for the asking. It is a gift for the taking. So whether you are facing old age, sickness, divorce, the end of a relationship, fear of the unknown , career uncertainties, insecurity or isolation, accept this gift from God. Move into that "peaceful center" and know that with God's help, you can handle whatever life throws at you. You will not only handle it, but maybe even triumph over it. No, you may not be able to handle it on your own; but with God's help, with Christ's peace, you can handle it, maybe even with dignity and grace. Pray for that "peaceful center." Ask for it! For whoever seeks finds. Whoever asks receives. Whoever knocks will find the door opening. It is probably already there, way down deep, way out of consciousness, waiting to be tapped. Find it! Use it! Live in it!

BALANCED

Render to Caesar the things that are Caesar's and to God the things that are God's.

                                                    Matthew 22

If you have never been the target of a stalker, you have missed one of life's scariest adventures. As some of you know, I had to deal with a stalker who fixated on me for about eight years when I was pastor of the Cathedral. The worst moment came when he pulled a ten-inch knife on me in the Cathedral itself, threatening to kill me if a homily welcoming anyone and everyone were given again! When I first went to the Cathedral in 1983, it was about to close. The membership had dropped to about one hundred people, mostly elderly women. We grew from those few members to about two thousand members by welcoming marginal Catholics, Catholics who had fallen away over the years, Catholics whose feelings had been hurt by insensitive clerics, divorced Catholics, gay and lesbian Catholics, and anyone else who traditionally did not feel welcome in our parishes. The stalker was especially angry about our welcome to divorced and gay Catholics. Several times during Mass he papered cars outside with hateful pamphlets ranting against me. For several months he paraded up and down in front of the Cathedral carrying a large sign which read "welcome to the church of Satan." I was in court with him five times for violating restraining orders to stay away from me and the Cathedral.

I also had another stalker — a different kind of one — a secret one, a very conservative priest, who wanted to catch me in my speech. He used to arrive for Mass late and take a seat in the very back with his yellow pad. He would take notes and leave again before Mass was over. Foolishly, I thought at first that he was just there to gather good sermon tips. I found out only later that he was looking for heretical statements so that he could report me to the Pope's representative in Washington. He was also the unnamed reporter for an archconservative group who published an anonymous, hateful "white paper," a booklet attacking the work of several priests in the diocese.

Jesus was the target of some of the same sort of stalking during his ministry. People from his own town of Nazareth dragged him out of the pulpit after one of his sermons and tried to throw him over a cliff because he was saying things like 'God loves Gentiles as much as Jews." Luke's gospel reads in Chapter 11: "the scribes and Pharisees began to act with hostility toward him and to interrogate him about many things, for they were plotting to catch him at something he might say."

They are at it again in today's gospel. "The Pharisees went off and plotted how they might trap him in speech." One of their tactics was to butter him up so that he would talk more. They do it in today's gospel. "We know that you are a truthful man and that you teach the way of God in

54

accordance with the truth." After schmoozing Jesus with that line, they set the trap. They asked him a question that, no matter how he answered it, would hang him. "Is it lawful to pay taxes to Caesar or not?" If he said "yes," he would alienate the Jews who hated the Roman Emperor and all Romans, seeing them as pagan Gentiles who had occupied their Jewish country in a war. If Jesus said "no," he would be accused of being a traitor to his country. Jesus cleverly side-stepped their trap by saying, "Give to Caesar what is Caesar's, but give to God what it God's."

Many of Jesus' best teaching comes forth on occasions like these. When the Pharisees gossiped that Jesus hung out with prostitutes and sinners, Jesus told the story of the Prodigal Son. When they tried to find a way out of loving Gentiles, he told the story of the Good Samaritan. When they tried to make him choose between religion and the state, he gave us today's memorable line. "Give to Caesar what is Caesar's, but give to God what is God's." For us, Jesus balances our duty to be good citizens and good Christians. It's not one or the other. It's about balance. It's both!

I just got back from giving a retreat to fifty priests in the diocese of Birmingham, Alabama. I, too, spoke about balance. A priest must be two things: good and good at what he does! He must work on one hand to become a holy, healthy and happy person. But that is not enough. He must work on the other hand to be an effective preacher of the gospel, presider at the celebration of the sacraments, and leader of the parish community. To be a good priest, he must be a good person and good at what he does!

As students here at Bellarmine, you too are challenged

by Jesus today to find this balance in your own life. You must do your spiritual work — you must pay attention to becoming a good person. You must do your professional work — you must pay attention to your studies so that you can become a competent person, effective in whatever profession you choose. You must, in a sense, "render to Caesar what is Caesar's and to God what is God's." You must keep God in your life as you prepare yourself to serve the world in your profession. The temptation that we priests face is that we might become so involved in our increasing workload as priests, neglecting our own spiritual lives, that some of us wake up one day with nothing left to give. The other temptation is to become overly absorbed in our pious practices and prayers as a way to avoid all the tension and chaos of dealing with real life and real people. A good lawyer, doctor, parent, teacher, musician, nurse, or whatever must also give attention to being both a good person, and giving good service to those who benefit from his or her daily work.

The lesson today? Love yourself and love your neighbor! Be a good person, and be good at what you do! "Render to Caesar the things that are Caesar's, but render to God the things that are God's." It's not either — or. It's both! Your teachers will help you in class. I hope to help you in here. So, come to church, and go to class. Be good, and be good at what you do.

FAKES

Be on guard against performing religious acts for people to see.

Matthew 6

One beautiful, sun-shiny day, a beautiful blond woman was driving through the mountains in a beautiful red Miata. The wind was blowing through her loose golden hair. The radio was cranked up on her favorite radio station. She was the picture of happiness as she made her way through the tight crooks and turns of the narrow mountain road. Coming from the other direction was a rough looking, overweight, middle aged man in a beat up old pick-up truck. As the red Miata passed the rusty old pick-up in one of the narrow turns, the rough looking man in the pick-up truck leaned out of his window and screamed as loud as he could at the woman in the convertible: "Pig!" The young woman was so angry that she stomped on the accelerator of her Miata and sped ahead. Just as she rounded the next bend, right there in the middle of the road, stood a huge pig! Unable to stop, she hit the pig head-on and totaled her car!

The word "hypocrite" appears three times in our gospel reading tonight. Like the word "pig" in the story I just told, the word "hypocrite" has two meanings. Originally the word "hypocrite" was a good word. Technically, it is simply the Greek word for "a professional actor in a play." Because of this passage, it became a word for a religious fake or a person who puts on a false pretense of virtue. Prayer, fasting and almsgiving — the pillars of Lenten observance — were time honored practices of the Jewish people. Jesus upholds them for his followers and they have become central to the Christian life as well. What Jesus is saying here is this: do these right things, but do them for the right reasons. Using language from the stage, what he says is this: when you pray, fast and give alms, don't play games!

(1) "When you give alms, do it quietly and without fanfare, unlike actors working for applause." Sometimes when people went to the synagogue to make a donation to the poor, they would almost hold a press conference so everybody would know about it. Right thing! Wrong reason! (2) "When you pray, don't do it in such a way that it will draw attention to yourself, just to impress people as an actor does." There were set times of prayer at the time of Jesus. Some people made sure they were in the right place at the right time so that they could drop to their knees in public and be noticed for their piety. Right thing! Wrong reason! (3) "When you fast, don't go around bragging about all you're giving up." Fasting back then was serious business. It would often leave you looking pale. Some people, though, took a short cut; they powdered their faces like actors so that people would **think** they were fasting. That way they could get credit for fasting, without actually doing it. All these people took good things (prayer, fasting and almsgiving) and did them for all the wrong reasons. Instead of being good, they settled for looking good.

We would never do that, would we? Unfortunately, even today we need to hear this reading. That's why the church puts this reading in front of us every Ash Wednesday! It's sort of a Lenten warning label because there is still much religious silliness and game playing in Lent. For instance, we are challenged to fast during Lent. Many go on a crash diet, not so that they can give the food they gave up to the poor, but so they will lose weight for the upcoming summer bathing suit. Hypocrisy! Dieting is not fasting! As a penance for our sins, we are challenged to abstain from meat on Ash Wednesday, Good Friday and all the Fridays of Lent. It is **supposed** to hurt a little. What do we do? We go out and buy shrimp cocktail, lobster tail, steamed clams, or oysters on the half shell, never daring to eat a hot dog or slice of bologna, and somehow comfort ourselves with the idea that we are actually doing God some big favor! Hypocrisy! Trading expensive shellfish and imported fish for meat cannot be called abstaining! Going around blabbing about what you're giving up for Lent and drawing attention to it is also hypocritical, Lenten play-acting!

My advice for Lent? Forget the legalistic religious game-playing, and simply get into the spirit of Lent. Simplify your life. Stop running around like a chicken with its head cut off! Focus less on your own needs and more on the needs of others. Cut back on food, pass on that expensive dinner, eat something simple, and use the money to feed the poor. Be more aware of God by spending more time with him and less on entertainment. Just sitting in the presence of God for a few minutes each day may be the best kind of private prayer. When you go to church, go to church! Focus your attention on praying with a group.

*Be on guard against performing religious acts for
people to see.*

Blessed are the poor of heart — blessed are those who
do the right thing for the right reason.

CALLED TO LOVE

LOVE

Each of them received a full day's pay.

Matthew 20

I grew up with some pretty strange ideas about God. I believed that if you're good to God, God will be good to you. I believed that God loves us when we're good, quits loving us when we are bad, and starts loving us again when we shape up. I never knew for sure whether I'd fly or fry if I died. Come to think of it, I never really liked God all that much. I was scared of God, so I tried to be as good as I could. No matter how hard I tried, I never felt good enough for God.

This was my idea of God until I was about thirty-two years old. By that time I had been a priest for about five years. It was during that year, 1975, that I had one of those life-changing breakthroughs in my thinking. It came to me in a very vivid dream. It changed my spiritual life for good. I dreamed one night that I was sitting on top of a short mountain — a high mound, really. It was covered with green grass, but no trees or plants grew there. I was sitting in one of those cheap aluminum lawn chairs. God was sitting beside me in another cheap lawn chair. We were both smoking King Edward cigars and watching the sun go down. He didn't say anything. I knew who sat beside me, but I was afraid to look over. We sat peacefully in silence, watching the sun go down, blowing smoke from our cheap cigars. Finally, after some time had gone by, God leaned over and whispered to me, "Ron! Isn't this wonderful?" I woke up after that dream with a feeling that I had experienced total acceptance, just as I am, flaws and all. That day, I traded in my judgmental God who lived out there, somewhere, for a partner-friend God who lived around and within me! It felt incredibly good. The first change I noticed after this dream was that it seemed my eyes were opened to the beauty of the parables that Jesus gave us. It was like I finally "got it!"

Today's parable about the vineyard owner is one of those life-changing stories. The first thing you need to know about this story is that it is not advice about how to run a business. It is about God and how God operates toward us. The point of the story is not about our love for God, but about God's love for us. God is the vineyard owner. We are the workers. Jesus tells us that God is like that recklessly generous vineyard owner. Some of us have worked for God all our lives, some once in a while and others hardly at all. Regardless of what we do or don't do, at the end of the day, God loves us all — 100%. God cannot love us all unconditionally and also love some more than others. It's about what God does for us, not about what we do for God.

So we can get it, there are many other parables that make the same point about God's crazy, generous love. Jesus sort of repeats himself for emphasis. There is the story of the man with two sons. One son stayed home and followed all the rules. The other son asked for his inheritance before his father died, blew it on sexual escapades, got down with the pigs, and had to come crawling home. Guess what? When he got home, his doting father threw a party. He loved both of his sons, regardless of what they did or did not do. What the prodigal son did was self-defeating and hurtful to his father, but the father did not withhold his love because of it. Jesus wants to tell us that God is like that! Then there is the story about the shepherd who has one hundred sheep. Ninety-nine of the sheep did what good sheep do. One wandered away, got in trouble, and had to be rescued. Guess what? The shepherd goes looking for that lost sheep, rescues him from his foolishness, and throws a party when he finds him. Jesus tells us that God is like that!

These stories were told by Jesus to teach us what God is like. The message behind them is the very message that Jesus came into the world to deliver from God. This message is what we call "the good news." It is amazing to me that so many people who call themselves "Christian" and "Catholic" have never really heard it. It is as if they never got beyond the packaging of religion and found the prize inside all the language, forms, laws, and customs. What is the "good news?" What is the essence of Jesus' message? It is simply this, told in a hundred ways: God loves you, no ands, ifs or buts about it, no matter what you have done or failed to do! That's it! That's the basic message! That is the heart of the matter! That's the kernel of truth.

Oh, yes, it does make a difference what you do and fail to do, but God's love for you does not depend on it. You may offend God, hurt others, do incredible damage to yourself, and refuse to love God back, but God does not quit loving you because of it. For those who think they must be good before God can love them, I remind them of these words, "While we were still sinners, Jesus died for us!" For those who think they must earn God's love, I remind them of today's gospel story. "At the end of the day, all received a full day's pay."

Many of you are, or will be, going through a reassessment of your childhood religion. It is part of being a young adult. Some of you will reject the religion of your childhood. Others will trade in their childhood religion for a more adult faith. My prayer for you is that you will have a moment of grace, maybe even a King Edward cigar kind of dream, when you let go of that distorted understanding of God that keeps God out there at arms length. Many experience God as a harsh, judgmental, and exacting despot. Like the IRS, this God is avoided as much as possible. May you discover the **true** God, the God in the parables that Jesus taught, a God who loves us all unconditionally, in spite of our sins, failures, and self-defeating stupidities. I love preaching this message. I have given my life to preach this message. My message to you today is the message that Jesus came to deliver: you are loved, period — no ands, ifs or buts about it — whether you feel loveable, or others think you are loveable, no matter what you've done or failed to do. This is the gospel! This is the essence of our religion! This is what Jesus died to tell us! This is the buried treasure. This is the pearl of great price! All God wants is for us to do is accept it, bask in it, and let it change our lives!

Each of them received a full day's pay.

64

CONNECTED

❖ ✠ ❖ ✠ ❖ ✠ ❖

Not too long ago I decided to take a couple of weeks of my vacation time. It was one of those "stay home" vacations. I slept late, shoveled out my house, mowed grass, cleaned out the basement, visited my family, planted the flower pots on the deck, and rebuilt the little fountain I have in my back yard. I had an old fountain, really part of a much larger fountain, which was so shallow that I had to watch it very carefully because if the water got too low, the pump motor would burn out. It was an aggravation to keep on eye on, so I moved the old fountain and built another one. I stacked the old fountain near a beautiful flowering shrub that I had been nursing for three years. The ground was too soft, so it fell over and crushed part of that shrub that I had been babying, breaking one of the main branches. I tried to save it, but it was too late. It had been severed from the main trunk. By the next day, the broken limb was withered so badly from the loss of vital sap from the main trunk that I had to cut it off and throw it away.

Just as a branch cannot bear fruit on its own unless it remains on the vine, so neither can you unless you remain in Jesus.

Jesus was familiar with the image of God as a gardener. In today's gospel, Jesus claims to be the true vine and says that we, his disciples, are the branches drawing life from him. The relationship is intimate and essential. The branches must be attached to the vine or else they will wither and die. We, his disciples, must remain united with him in order to live and to thrive.

This intimate connection between God and ourselves is nothing new. We have no mean, stern, aloof, cold and moody God who isolates himself in some far off heaven, aggravated by most of what we do. We have a God who likes to snuggle. He craves "being with" us. Even in the garden of Eden, God is pictured walking in the garden with Adam and Eve. The prophets often spoke about our relationship with God as a marriage, using lots of sexual images. If you don't believe me, read the Song of Songs. Passages from that book are often chosen for readings at weddings. Other Old Testament readings tell us that even when we "whore around" with other gods, our God remains faithful to us, taking us back again and again. The ancient Jews were not American Puritans. They spoke of God as "El Kane," the passionate young lover in heat, with us as the target of his "ah-ha-bah," his "aroused love." Even when we are frigid in our response to his advances, he never stops trying. If that were not enough, God crawls inside human flesh in the person of Jesus. At his birth, Jesus was called "Emmanuel," meaning "God with us!" This Jesus, God in the flesh, talked often about the intimate relationship between God and us. Last week he spoke of himself as the good shepherd and us as his sheep. This shepherd lays down his life for us. During Lent, we heard Jesus call himself "living water," a well that never runs dry. No one can live without water. This week he calls himself "the vine" and us "the branches." He gives himself to us — his body and blood as "bread and wine" — and asks us to "feed on" him. This Jesus "walks with" his disciples on the road to Emmaus. After his ascension to heaven he makes us temples of his Holy Spirit, living within us. Yes, we have a God who craves "being with" us, a God who is driven to snuggle!

My friends, we are challenged by today's gospel to consider our intimate connection to God. The gospel today uses the phrase "remain in me" five times. When people speak of God, they often (arrogantly) put themselves in the center of the universe, with God out there on hold somewhere. They speak as if we can ignore God and keep him at arms' length, out of our lives when we feel like it. We are not the center of the universe. God is! We can ignore God, and life can go on, but if God ignored us for one second, we would cease to be. It's not us who choose God, it is God who chooses us first. The relationship is already there. We can ignore it, cut ourselves off and try to go our own way, **or** we can wake up to God, realize our dependence on God, and draw life from him like branches on a vine. We have a choice. Our choice has implications.

Like the broken limb in my back yard that was ripped from the main shrub and ended up withering by the next morning, apart from God we cannot make it. We already have a relationship with God because God initiated it. To make it life-giving, life-enhancing and life-sustaining, we must first of all be conscious of the relationship we already have! The ancient Jews wore bible quotes in tiny boxes on their foreheads to remind themselves. My favorite way of reminding myself is to have an on-going, all day, conversation with God. I do the formal prayer thing, of course, but my favorite way to pray is to picture God as walking with me "in the garden" and "on the road to Emmaus." I picture God as my roommate, my best friend, my confidant, and my constant companion. We chit chat all day long! The best dream I ever had was one with me and God smoking King Edward cigars in cheap lawn chairs, watching the sun go down from a mountain top.

I know from personal experience that when I live consciously aware of my intimate connection to God, when I "remain in him" and his "words remain in me," I can ask for what I need, and it will be given to me. And more often than not, more than I need is given to me. I also know that when I have let my intimate connection to God slip from my awareness and try to "go it alone," my life gets out of sync very quickly.

"Remain in me as I remain in you," Jesus says to us today. Like branches that feed on the vine and draw life and strength from it, we are now invited to "feed on" the body and blood of Jesus and draw life and strength from him. As the great saints used to say about the Eucharist, over time "we become what we eat." What we do in here gives us strength for what we do out there. Now that we have "fed on" the Word of God, let us "feed on" the Body and Blood of Jesus and on the community of believers that gather with us. We do all this to help us remember and be conscious of our intimate connection with God and with each other.

Remain in me, as I remain in you. Just as a branch cannot bear fruit on its own unless it remains on the vine, so neither can you unless you remain in me.

INCLUDED

When Jesus was born . . . behold, magi from the east arrived . . . to do him homage.

Matthew 2

Let's not get bogged down in the details — star, magi, gold, frankincense, and myrrh! When it comes right down to it, details are not all that important. They are just part of some elaborate packaging! So let's rip through the packaging and get to the real meat of this feast. The essential message, the kernel of truth, the pressing fact this story is trying to communicate is simply this: God loves everybody! Do you really understand what I'm saying here? God loves every human being on this planet — always has and always will! Not just Jews, but everybody! Not just Catholics, but everybody! Not just Baptists, but everybody! Christians! Jews! Muslims! Hindus! Atheists! Everybody!!!!!! Everybody!

Unfortunately, that's not what many of us believe. That's not what many of us were taught. That's certainly not what many of us live by! The very idea of Gentiles showing up to do homage to the newborn Jewish Messiah was outrageous back then because the Jewish people believed that God loved Jews and hated Gentiles. The real message behind today's mind-blowing story is that God's love is not confined by the boundaries we humans place around it. God's love has no boundaries!

This Jewish baby, God's only Son, who in today's gospel story welcomes even Gentile visitors, grew up and continued to tear down the walls people had erected around God's love. This Jewish baby, God's only Son, who welcomes even Gentile visitors today, reached out and embraced Jews and Gentiles, outcasts and sinners, diseased and forgotten, good and bad alike. This Jewish baby, God's only Son, who welcomes even Gentile visitors today, commands that we, who have received this unconditional and undeserved love, do the same — that we reverence every human being, no exceptions, even our enemies. In other words, we are challenged today to take on the mind of God himself! We must think as God thinks! Today we are challenged to have the heart of Jesus, the heart of God, a heart big enough and with room enough to hold everybody!

We are challenged by this feast to have a "catholic" heart. You heard me, a "catholic" heart. The word "catholic" means universal and inclusive. But how can we open our hearts wide enough to hold the variety and difference we bump into each day? How do we open our minds enough to appreciate and enjoy the incredible range of perspectives, without the need to convert, subdue, attack and change them? How can we resist the need to recreate the world in our own image and likeness instead of enjoying it as it is, as God created it, incredibly beautiful in all its diversity? How do we start molding such a heart?

First, we start by loving ourselves, our whole selves,

every part of ourselves. If God can love us *as we are,* then we must learn to love ourselves *as we are!* If we cannot love ourselves, with all our faults, contradictions, and limitations, there is no hope at all that we can accept those things in others. If we cannot embrace and nurture every part of ourselves, we will never be able to embrace and nurture those same wounds in others.

Second, to have a heart that can hold a place open for others, especially those whom the world rejects, means that we must be people of great courage, people of great guts and principle. Rejection is the price of compassion. Jesus was condemned to death for making room in his heart, for making room in God's kingdom, for embracing all people no matter what shape or condition they were in — even those who could not love him back, even his enemies! It takes great courage to live in this world with a heart that big, that generous, and that compassionate! It takes great courage to be "catholic" in the best sense of that word!

Today, on this Feast of the Epiphany, we celebrate God's unconditional embrace of all human beings — the good and the bad, the deserving and undeserving, the acceptable and the unacceptable, everybody! I mean everybody!

How much room is there in your heart? Whom do you allow in? Whom do you exclude? An enlargement of your heart this year will be the surest sign of spiritual health. May your heart enlarge to the point where you can love and appreciate all your human qualities and all the human qualities of the people around you. May your heart open up until you can call yourself "catholic" in the truest sense of the word!

DIFFERENCES

*When the disciples James and John saw this they asked,
"Lord, do you want us to call down fire from heaven to
consume them?"*

Luke 9

◈ ✠ ◈ ✠ ◈ ✠ ◈

There is an old story about a far distant country, somewhere to the north of Afghanistan. In this country there was
a city inhabited entirely by the blind. One day the news came
that an elephant was passing outside the walls of this city.

The citizens called a meeting and decided to send a del-
egation of three men outside the gates so that they could report back what an elephant was. In due course, the three men
left the town and stumbled forwards until they eventually
found the elephant. Each of the three reached out, felt the
animal with their hands, then they all headed back to the
town as quickly as they could to report what they had felt.

The first man said: "An elephant is a marvelous creature! It is like a vast snake, but it can stand vertically upright
in the air!" The second man was indignant at hearing this:
"What nonsense!" he said. "This man is misleading you. I
felt the elephant and what it most resembles is a pillar. It is
firm and solid, and however hard you push against it, you
could never knock it over." The third man shook his head

and said: "Both these men are liars! I felt the elephant and it resembles a broad *pankah*. It is wide and flat and leathery and when you shake it, it wobbles around like the sail of a *dhow*." All three men stuck by their stories and for the rest of their lives they refused to speak to each other. Each one professed that he — and only he — knew the whole truth.

Now of course, all three of these blind men had a measure of insight. The first man felt the trunk of the elephant, the second the leg, the third the ear. All had part of the truth, but not one of them had even begun to grasp the totality or the greatness of the beast they had encountered. If only they had listened to one another and meditated on the different facets of the elephant, they might have realized the true nature of the beast. But they were too proud and instead preferred to keep to their own half-truths.

So it is with us. Muslims see God one way, the Hindus have a different conception, and we Christians have a third. To us, all our different visions seem incompatible and irreconcilable. But what we forget is that before God we are like blind men stumbling around in total blackness. I love this story, and it seems to fit the situation tonight. We live in a world where difference is often the source of mistrust, division, and even hatred — all because we experience reality from varied perspectives.

I chose our gospel story tonight because it seems to be so on target! Even the holy apostles, the original disciples of Jesus, could not understand how anything good could happen outside their circle. John, known for his lofty words about love, came up to Jesus one day after noticing that other groups were doing wonderful things. He told Jesus that he and others had tried to stop them "because they were not of our company," because they were not like us! Jesus tells them, "Do not stop them, for anyone who is not against us, is for us!" When they wanted to enter a Samaritan town, the Samaritans snubbed them and would not welcome them. Jesus and his group were Jews. Jews hated Samaritans. Even though they were Jewish in their roots, they had intermarried with Gentiles. They were different, religiously and ethnically! Because of the snub, James and John suggested that they "call fire down from heaven and destroy them." Jesus turned to them and reprimanded them. This story has much to teach our modern world, riddled with religious wars!

Many people seem to be unable to deal with all this variety and insist that unity is possible only when everybody else conforms to their way of being, seeing, believing, and doing. That is not only impossible, it is not even good. We hear a lot these days about the call for tolerance. Tolerance means simply putting up with others. That may be the next step, but that is not the whole answer either. I like this story because it points us toward the only possible path to unity: appreciating, respecting, and celebrating all our marvelous diversity. Variety **IS** the spice of life! We will never have unity until we can move from our "points of view" to a "viewing point." From there we can appreciate other points of view, while holding on to our own! Unity does not necessarily mean uniformity! If we don't "get this" we will keep on having Crusades, Inquisitions, sexism, racism, ageism, Columbine massacres and God knows what else. Advances in communications and travel bring us ever closer together. We neglect the work of peacemaking at our own peril.

RECEPTIVE

. . . no one pours new wine into old wineskins.

Mark 2

It is good, from time to time, to stop and remember just who **accepted** Jesus and just who **rejected** Jesus. Amazingly, it was religious people who rejected Jesus and so-called "sinners" who welcomed him.

Jesus came with a refreshing new message, a convincing message of love and forgiveness from God himself. The message was simply this: God loves us without condition, no ands, ifs or buts about it. The sick heard his message and flocked to him. People believed back then that all illness was God's punishment for sin. People who were sick presumed that God hated them. Jesus told them differently. Wealth was seen as a sign of God's favor. If you were rich, it was a sign that God loved you. If you were poor, it was a sign of God's displeasure. Jesus told them differently. The poor heard his message and flocked to him. Prostitutes, tax-collectors, foreigners, and church drop-outs heard his message and flocked to him. They too assumed that God hated them. By eating with them, drinking with them, and visiting their homes, Jesus tells them not just in word, but in deed: "God loves you without condition." Jesus exuded God's unbelievably generous love for all of people.

This fresh new message is the "new wine" of the parable. "New wine" requires "new wineskins." In Jesus' day, wine was fermented in animal skins. Since the fermenting wine bubbles and churns, it needs a soft flexible container: a new, fresh wineskin. Were you to put new wine into brittle old skins, the fermenting action of the new wine could cause the brittle, old skin to break. The message? A new message needs a new mind. Those whose minds were "open" accepted Jesus and celebrated his "new message."

Those whose minds were closed rejected Jesus and his fresh new message. The religious authorities were afraid of this "new message." Their minds were the brittle old wineskins. They had the world by the tail. They liked the way things were. They had a vested interest in the elaborate structure that previous generations had erected around religion. Especially around the sin business, there was money to be made. Instead of God being alive in their hearts, God was a name found in a rule book. It was as if they had domesticated God, preserved him in formaldehyde, and put him on the shelf. Religion had become an exclusive club for the self-righteous who had fallen into worshiping the forms of religion. Jesus' new message upset that apple cart. Disliking the message, they hated, plotted against, attacked, and finally killed the messenger. Jesus was crucified by those who had a stake in the *status quo*. "You can't put new wine into brittle, old wineskins." You can't put new ideas into brittle, worn, inflexible, closed minds.

The process of opening your mind and heart to God is called *metanoia*. It was the first word out of Jesus' mouth as he began preaching. *Metanoia* is a radical, life changing, 180° turn in thinking. Change the way you think! Change the way you look at things! Change the way you view people! Without that change of mind and heart, you can not understand what Jesus is saying.

What about you? What kind of mind and heart do you have? Are they open and flexible and fresh? Are they closed, rigid, and brittle? You know it has nothing to do with age. It's a choice one makes. I know some people in their nineties who have faced unbelievable pain and disappointment and yet are happy and young at heart. They are still interested and interesting, flexible in their thinking. I know some people in their twenties who have already emotionally shut down, bitter and angry, rigid in their thinking.

God is alive and well. God is doing marvelous things in our midst even today. Miracles are happening all around us. Only those with eyes to see them, see them! Only those with open hearts, receive them! God is not dead! We are! Most of the world's problems can be fixed only with a change of heart. Social scientists, for instance, tell us there is enough food on this planet to feed everybody. We just don't have the will yet to do it! Only a change of heart will solve the hunger problem. Racism and religious bigotry are attitude problems. Only a change of heart will eliminate them. The way we treat the elderly in this country is a scandal. Only a change of heart will fix it. Grudges, resentments, and hatreds drag us down spiritually, physically, and emotionally. Only a change of heart will heal them.

Jesus knew quite well that he was coming with a message that was startlingly new. He also knew that his way of life was quite different from that taught by the rabbis of his day. He knew how difficult it is for human minds to accept and entertain new truth. To be alive is to change, and to be fully alive is to change often. Dr. M. Scott Peck in his book *The Road Less Traveled* puts it best. He says that when we have the world like we want it and everything is just fine, something happens, a new reality comes along. We may lose our spouse, lover, or closest friend. We may lose our job or be diagnosed with a terrible disease. We may have an unwanted pregnancy. We may kick and scream and resist this new reality with everything in our bodies. We may think that if we don't like it enough, it will go away. We may even crusade against it, condemn it as false, heretical, the work of the devil, or just pretend it didn't happen. When we do all that, we shut out minds and our hearts. We grow bitter and resentful. When we do that we shut out the possibility of receiving something equally as good or better into our lives. God only knows how many wonderful things we have probably missed when we have refused to deal with painful realities.

You cannot put new wine into old wine skins. Jesus is shut out by a closed mind and a closed heart! Unless we become like little children (curious, open, and trusting), Jesus says, we cannot enter the kingdom of God. Trust God! Keep your mind open and your heart flexible! You never know what new wonders God has in store for you on the other side of a so-called "tragedy."

Forgiveness

Wrath and anger are hateful things, yet the sinner hugs them tight.

Sirach 27

I always get a big laugh when I stumble onto that program that features "The Strongest Man on Earth" competition. It's sort of like those log rolling, chain saw wielding, ax swinging lumber-jack contests up north somewhere, but different. In this contest, obscenely huge men carry or drag things like massive blocks of concrete in an awkward looking hundred yard dash. They sweat. They groan. They growl. They grimace and stagger in pain. They are well trained athletes, but some of the things they carry, drag and push are ridiculous. It almost hurts to watch them.

A grudge is like that! A grudge is like carrying around a big block of concrete in your head and your heart. Carrying grudges wears you out. Many people carry the back-breaking weight of a grudge, in pain, for years and years. Every time they think of the one they have a grudge against, they rehearse and obsess about the other's guilt and their innocence. The more they rehearse and obsess, the more they remember. The more they remember, the more they obsess, until a vicious cycle is set up. They bore their friends in the retelling of it. Before long, the grudge owns them. "Wrath and hatred are hateful things, but the sinner hugs them tight." I have met hundreds of people who have done that. I am one of them!

My father was a psychologically abusive "rageaholic." He threw daily, curse-filled, demeaning, temper tantrums. The rage, directed at both us kids and my mother, was a constant in our family as long as I can remember. Psychological abuse leaves no external marks, but believe me, the wounds are nonetheless deep. I left home for good after one of his rages when I was half-way through seminary. Back then, most seminarians went home during the holidays and during the summers. I stayed here in Louisville, rented a basement apartment, and worked three summer jobs to support myself during my last six years in the seminary. I stayed clear of him as much as possible until I was ordained, and for seventeen years afterwards, as a priest. Even though I was not around him much, I carried around resentment toward him in my heart — a heavy stinking bag of resentment that I couldn't seem to let go of! When I heard others' confessions, I insisted that they forgive the people in their lives. The words of the Lord's Prayer (forgive us as we forgive others) stuck in my throat every time I said it. I even preached eloquent sermons to others on forgiveness. But, all the while, I could not forgive my own father. The bag of resentments and grudges finally got so heavy and stank so badly that I finally decided to give it up. I knew I could not do it by myself. I began to pray that God would help me. I began to read as much as I could about the process of forgiveness. Several months later, it came to me, in what had to be a moment of grace, that forgiveness had to come from me and it had to be a unilateral forgiveness. I knew I had to forgive him whether he ever admitted wrong or ever apologized to me. I knew I had to do it for my own good, before he died, or I would carry that grudge for the rest of my life.

I called my father up one day and told him I was coming down and bringing dinner. I planned to talk to him after dinner. I chickened out. I ended up doing that three times before I finally had the courage to open my mouth. God was indeed helping me, because what I intended to say and what I actually said were different. I had planned to remind him about all the awful things he had done and said, but what actually came out of my mouth was this: "You know, we have never really liked each other. I want to get it behind us once and for all. I have been so mad at you for so long for what you did to hurt me as a child that I have never told you "thanks" for the good things you have done. Then (this had to have come from God), I said, "I'm sorry for all the times I have been cold and punishing toward you for all you did back then." Yes, I admitted to myself and to him, that taking offense is just as bad as giving offense. I left there that night feeling lighter and freer than I have ever felt in my life. It was June 7, 1987, 6:30 p. m. I will always be thankful that I did that. He died a few years ago. We never mentioned it again, we never got any closer, but I didn't need to. I had finally finished grieving over not having the father I needed and wanted, and learned to accept the one I had. Now I can look at his grave without remorse, without resentment, and even with some compassion. He is free now and so am I!

Who, in your life, have you not yet forgiven? A parent?

An old boyfriend? An old girlfriend? A former spouse? A teacher? A friend? Is it still eating at you, controlling your thinking, and blocking your heart? If it is, God wants you to let go of it, not for their good or His good, but for **your** good! With God's help, you can cut yourself free of your bag of stinking resentment, anger, and wrath, if you really want to! It doesn't matter who is wrong or how many incidents you can count. It doesn't matter whether justice is done or whether they even admit they were wrong. It can be unilateral!

Today's parable tells us that if God can forgive us our zillion dollar debt to him, then we can forgive the piddly little debts others owe us. We share in the sins that nailed Jesus to the cross, yet he has forgiven us. Can we not, then, forgive the slights and hurts that others inflict on us? We are loved without condition by God; we need to love each other without condition. What used to scare me the most when I could not forgive my father were the words of the Lords Prayer, "Forgive me my sins **as I forgive** those who sin against me." I was actually asking God to withhold his forgiveness from me until I could forgive those around me! Now that was a scary thought!

My friends, forgive, even if it takes a while, even if you have been offended seventy times seven times. Do it for your own good, if for no other reason! It will lighten your load, give you a clean heart, and make you more appreciative of God's forgiveness and love that we celebrate here in this Eucharist!

FAMILY

The child grew and became strong, filled with wisdom; and the favor of God was upon him.

Luke 2

Today's feast, the feast of the Holy Family, has come up thirty times since I have been doing my preaching thing! All thirty times I've had a problem coming up with something to say on this day. A lot of it has to do with the fact that devotion to the Holy Family was a big thing when I was going through Catholic grade school. My beloved nun teachers used to measure all family life against the standard of the Holy Family of Nazareth. Well, when you come from a family like mine, you not only never measured up, you never even got close, leaving you feeling totally defective. I grew up in the country. There were nine of us. It was sort of a cross between the Waltons and *Psycho*! That's why I have always been a little uncomfortable about this feast and always at a loss for words — this **perfect** little family from Nazareth seemed to have little in common with my **imperfect** little family from Rhodelia!

As a result of all this, I approach this Feast of the Holy Family with caution. Some of you here may have a perfect, cozy family. If you do, I am happy for you. But I also know that there are many more "families" that do not measure up to that standard, and this feast is supposed to inspire those families as well — single parent families, adoptive families, refugee and immigrant families, blended families, foster care families, grandparent families, gay and lesbian families, absent parent families, and those of us who have created a circle of friends as a substitute family. So whether you were raised on Walton's Mountain, raised in the Little House on the Prairie, raised in a Cleaver household, raised by the Brady Bunch, or even raised by a bunch of wolves, this feast has **something** to inspire you!

On closer look, maybe we have over-glamorized and idealized this "holy family of Nazareth." After all, even though it was by the power of the Holy Spirit, Mary was found to be "with child" before she was legally married, when she was only engaged to Joseph. That would make Joseph, not the real father! (Today, I guess they would be dragged to some talk show and Joseph would be forced to submit to a paternity test!) Jesus was born outside the home, in a barn. Some might consider this poor planning by an inexperienced, young, teen-aged mother. Mary and Joseph were refugees in a foreign country for a while, when a murderous maniac started stalking them. Jesus was on the "missing child" list for a few days when he got lost on a trip to the big city. Mary thought he was with Joseph. Joseph thought he was with Mary. On the trip home, he was missing for a day before they even noticed he was gone, and started to looked for him. Embarrassed and panic stricken, they had to go back and search for him. Tradition tells us that Joseph died early, leaving Mary a widow and a single parent. After a sermon in his hometown, the congregation tried to throw Jesus over a cliff. At one point, Jesus' extended family tried to have him committed, thinking he had lost his mind. Finally, Jesus, the only son of a widowed mother, was arrested and executed as a common criminal! Then, with her real family gone, Mary ends up being taken in by her dead son's close friend, John.

My theory is that God arranged all this so that all of us who come from less-than-perfect-families can find something to identify with in this "holy family." Whatever form of family we find ourselves in tonight, the "family values" outlined in tonight's readings are meant to inspire us as we live and contribute to our families, whatever shape they may have taken. These readings tell us to "honor our parents," "take care of them when they are old," "be compassionate, kind, humble, gentle, patient, loving, thankful, and forgiving toward our family members." The gospel challenges us, further, to "fulfill all the prescriptions of the law of the Lord" and "to grow and become strong, filled with wisdom." These are the "family values" that all of us are called to live, no matter what kind of family we find ourselves in tonight!

COMPASSION

*Moved with pity, Jesus stretched out his hand, touched
the leper and said to him, " . . . be made clean!"*

Mark 1

One of the best things about being a priest is helping
people die! I know it sounds weird, but it's true. Because
you are around it so much, you can often actually be very
helpful to those who are dying and to those who grieve for
them. The most memorable death I have witnessed happened
at University Hospital a few years ago. I was called to the
hospital to visit an eleven year old boy who was just brought
in with critical burns all over his body. In fact, the only places
not burned were the very tips of his fingers and the bottoms
of his feet. He and his friend had lit a match while playing
on top of a large gas tank. In the explosion, his friend was
killed outright. About all the doctors could do was to wrap
the burns, dirt and all, sedate the boy, and wait. There was
no skin to graft. I made several trips over a ten-day period.
One night I went in and the nurses were in tears. They told
me that since the bandages could not be removed, they feared
that the boy was literally rotting under the bandages, maybe
even that maggots had begun to grow. But his heart was still
strong and they believed that he could go on living several
more days. The family had surrounded the boy all week,

whispering words of encouragement, telling him to hang on. The nurses advised me to go on home. Something told me not to go. I had remembered something I had read in pastoral counseling. I went into the room, took a deep breath and went to the head of the bed. Then I turned around and said to the family, "You have shown all week that you truly love Johnny. You have told him to hang in there. He has been trying to do as you say. Maybe it's time to tell him it's OK to let go." They looked at each other for a few minutes and then, beginning with the grandmother, all of them came one at a time to the head of the bed and began to pat his bandaged head and stroke his bandaged arms. They told him how much they loved him, how brave he had been, that it was alright to let go, and that God would be there to take care of him. After a few minutes, I left the room to give them privacy. I stood outside the room with the nurse. In about fifteen minutes, the nurse said, "I can't believe this!" The numbers on his monitor had begun to fall, little by little. In less than a half hour, the poor little boy died, surrounded by his family.

During this past summer alone, I helped two families make the decision to turn off the machines when all was lost for their loved ones. But my most heart wrenching experiences of death were with those six or seven who died of AIDS. I remember one young man I visited several times before he died. He was scared of God because he believed that God would not forgive him for his promiscuous lifestyle. I tried every way I knew how to let him know that God's love for us is unconditional. I used to quote a few lines from one of the Eucharistic Prayers for Mass. "When we were lost and could not find our way to you, you loved us more than ever." Abandoned by his family, unsure of God's love, in pain and skeleton-like, he died on a mattress on the floor in an ugly apartment in old Louisville. I helped another young man prepare for death over the phone. He lived in another state. His brother told me about him and asked if I would call and talk to him. We talked several times before he died. He, too, was facing death, wondering whether God could love him enough to forgive him. It was almost as if he were expecting hell. I don't know if he ever really and truly believed in God's love for him. He had once been a very handsome and talented young man. When he died, he was skin and bones, covered with sores, and crying in pain. His family was so embarrassed by him and his disease that they would not even tell the priest who did his funeral. I was depressed for weeks when I heard that he had died.

The AIDS of Jesus day was leprosy. Jesus is confronted by a leper in today's gospel. Our first reading told us how lepers were traditionally treated. The gospel tells us how Jesus treated them. Like AIDS sufferers today, the fate of the leper was tragic on three fronts: (1) there was progressive and intense physical pain; (2) there was the mental pain of being shunned by family and friends; (3) there was the spiritual horror of a popular theology which held that leprosy was a punishment from God for some sin the sick person had committed. Most died in pain, living in caves and cemeteries, cut off from their family and friends, believing that even God hated them. Because they did not have the diagnostic tools we have today, it's possible that some of them went to their death with nothing more than a bad case of eczema or psoriasis or some other chronic skin disease!

Jesus knew the old religious laws about not speaking to — much less touching — lepers. The leper knew it was illegal to come that close, much less speak to Jesus. Both Jesus and the leper knew that people believed that his condition was God's punishment. But Jesus not only allowed such outcasts (lepers, prostitutes, and many who were labeled "sinners') to approach him, he made it a point to seek them out! Like the shepherd who lost one of his sheep, he went looking for these people, not to condemn them, but to offer them a hug from God. For this kind of behavior Jesus was severely criticized by the religious people of his day. "This man welcomes sinners and even eats with them!" Even if Jesus had not been able to cure this leper, he would have worked a miracle by being compassionate toward him. It had probably been years since this poor human being had felt that kind of warmth and compassion from another person. This incredible compassion carried even more power since it came from a famous young man of God, the rabbi Jesus from Nazareth. Jesus not only healed the leper, but as a religious person, Jesus welcomed him back into the community of Israel.

My brothers and sisters, what we are talking about today is "compassion." The word "compassion" comes from the two Latin words *com* and *passio*, meaning "to suffer with." Jesus had a tender heart, the tender heart of God. When he saw the poor, the hungry, the sick, and the rejected, he was "moved with pity;" he "suffered with" them. As his followers, those chosen to carry on his work, we are called to adopt Jesus' attitude of acceptance and love for all people, especially those who have been shunned by others. We live in a world where it seems that tolerance for those on the edge of society drops daily. We need only to recall the incident at Columbine High, the Matthew Shepherd incident, and the continuation of racism to know that we live in a world where people who are different are teased, tortured, discriminated against, and even killed. We fear what we do not understand. We hate what we fear.

The only way to do "compassion" is to "reach out" to those who are excluded, exiled, and abused. As Jesus did in today's Gospel, we must reach across the ignorance and prejudice and hostility to those who live on the margins of our church and country and world. Jesus, who was the compassion of God in the flesh, searched them out, touched them and made them feel a part of the human family. As Christians, we are not called to tolerance, simply putting up with those who are marginalized. We are called to tear down the margins, to carry on the tradition of being God's compassion in the flesh.

Have you ever come to the defense of the defenseless? Have you every stopped a racist or homophobic joke? Have you judged those who suffer from AIDS? Do you judge, categorize, and resent the homeless, immigrants, or the handicapped without knowing much about them? Have you ever done anything to relieve their pain or help those who are in trouble? We are Christ's Body in the world. If the marginalized do not feel the compassion of Christ from us, from whom will they feel it? In a world where rudeness and crudeness, bigotry and hatred escalates almost daily, we really could be "the light of the world" and "salt of the earth,"

showing the world how to be truly "compassionate," something the world needs desperately. The world is healed, not
by some huge program, but by one compassionate gesture
at a time.

CALLED TO FIDELITY

ALWAYS

"Behold, I am with you always, until the end of time."
Matthew 28

I have **always** felt that God has been with me: when I was a child, when I was an adolescent, when I was a young adult, and especially now. I am acutely aware that this awareness is not something that I accomplished because I am holier than anyone else, but that it is simply a gift from God for which I am truly grateful. Even though I am intensely aware that I live and breathe in the presence of God, God is not in the habit of speaking directly to me, except maybe once. One night, in the months after I left the Cathedral, I was in a state of worry, anxiety, and fretfulness about what to do next with my life. Over several days I had worked myself into a lather. I was in one of those negative mind-chatter episodes when I tend to tell myself all the bad things that I can imagine. I was filing some papers when all of a sudden I heard someone say in a clear and distinct voice, "Don't worry!" I looked around to see if someone had sneaked up on me. No one! Then I looked at the TV to see if I had heard those words from the TV set. It was off! It didn't scare me. It was a very comforting voice. Did I need to hear it so badly that I imagined it? Maybe! But maybe not! All I know for sure was that a great peace came over me at that moment. It was very similar to those words in scripture that Jesus once spoke, "Fear is useless. What is needed is trust."

That happened only once, but I have always felt that Jesus has been with me throughout my life. When I was young, I was intensely aware of Jesus' presence in the tabernacle of my home church. So was everybody else! That awareness was so real that we went out of our way to drop into church whenever possible to pay Jesus a visit, just to say hi or ask for a favor. Men tipped their hats and people made the sign of the cross in their cars as they drove past the church. Every June, we even carried the Body of Christ in a gold holder, praying and singing to him as we walked around the track at Churchill Downs. Because so many people came to participate in that event, Churchill Downs was used because it was the biggest place the church could find back then.

As Catholics, we still believe that Jesus is indeed present in the Eucharistic Bread, but awareness of other ways that Jesus is present became popular after Vatican Council II, diminishing the intensity that once lived in the church around the presence of Jesus in the reserved sacrament. This new awareness centers around the presence of Jesus in the people of the church. We began to see ourselves as walking tabernacles, holding the presence of Jesus. Another renewed awareness centers around the presence of Jesus in the Holy Scriptures, maybe one of the biggest gifts of Vatican Council II. In fact, Vatican Council II says that Christ is present with us in the people of the church praying and singing, in the person of the priest in the celebration of the sacraments, in the proclamation of the holy scriptures, and especially in the Eucharistic species, the consecrated bread and wine at Mass.

But there are other ways as well. Some people experience the abiding presence of Christ in the beauty and majesty of nature, in the service of the poor and suffering, in the arts, in their spouses, children and friends, in still quiet moments when they are alone, even in times of great loss and the process of dying. "I am with you always, until the end of time?" Most certainly! As Elizabeth Barret Browning put it, "Earth's crammed with heaven, and every common bush afire with God." The poet Gerard Manley Hopkins puts it this way: "The world is charged with the grandeur of God." The Psalmist asks, "Where can I go from your spirit, from your presence where can I flee? If I go up to the heavens, you are there; if I sink to the nether world, you are present there. If I take the wings of the dawn, if I settle at the farthest limits of the sea, even there your hand shall guide me, your right hand hold me fast."

"I am with you always, until the end of time." These final words of Jesus to his disciples in today's gospel are also meant for us. The words of that old folk song : "You've got to walk that lonesome valley. You got to walk it all by yourself" are dead wrong. Jesus is indeed with us, with us in many, many ways. The problem is not that Jesus is not always with us.The problem is that we often have "eyes that see not and ears that hear not!" We are like the disciples on that first Easter evening, walking down the road with eyes downcast, unaware that Jesus walks with us. We have a God who walked with us in the garden at creation. We have a God who is married to us for better or worse. We have a God who became one of us in the person of Jesus Christ. We have a God who lives within us in the Holy Spirit. We have a God who invites us to be with him forever in paradise. We have a God who is with us always, till the end of the world and beyond. All we have to do is to wake up to his presence, bask in it, work with it, and look forward to enjoying that presence forever.

ATTENTION

. . . stay awake, for you know neither the day nor the hour.

Matthew 25

When I was a seminary student, there was a warning that circulated among the Louisville seminarians. This warning was repeated more and more often the closer we got to ordination. "You'd better not screw up or you'll end up in Somerset!" The Somerset assignment was a five-county mission parish the size of the state of Delaware. It was as far from Louisville as you could get in our diocese, and it had a reputation as the bishop's dumping ground for priest-malcontents and mischief-makers. Guess where **my** first assignment was? Somerset!

In my time the dreaded Father Buren was the pastor. Father Buren was a good priest, but he was known for chewing up associate pastors and spitting them out. After being made to stay in the rectory, day and night, for a month, I was becoming bored out of my mind. One Sunday afternoon, all the Masses being done, I went to the lake with some parish teenagers. When I got back I got a chewing out from Father Buren like I had never been chewed out before. Even though no one ever called the rectory on Sunday afternoon, he said he wanted me there "in case a sick call came in." Toward the end of the summer, though, I got a breather. The pastor decided to take a few days off.

"When the cat's away, the mice will play." I planned a party at the rectory, something that had obviously never ever been done in the history of that parish. The pastor left on Sunday and was "supposed" to return on Friday. On Thursday night, just about the time the party got rolling, the front door suddenly flew open and there, staring down at me, stood a gigantic, furious Father Buren. Stunned into a trance, I just stood there speechless. Caught "with my pants down," so to speak, after what seemed an eternity I managed to blurt out: "I thought you were coming home tomorrow!" In the iciest tone I have ever heard in my life, he said in a very deep voice: "I said I would be home **by** tomorrow." The party obviously died a premature death. To paraphrase the words of the gospel today, "This foolish virgin was caught with no oil in his lamp."

The parable we have just read is one of several parables about readiness. Whatever the original text and context of these parables, they stand as warnings against laxness on the part of Christians. The thrust here is not on prediction, so as to "get ready," but on "being ready." The parable tells us to focus, not on the future, but on the present; not on dying, but on living. As one parable puts it: "let your belts be fastened around your waists and your lamps be burning brightly." They remind us that one who goes through life alert, awake, and on his toes need not worry about "the day or the hour." They remind us that if one is truly engaged with life, one does not have to worry about preparing for death. No, this parable is not about getting ready, but about being ready; about consciously living a life of attention, focus, and purpose — the opposite of snoozing and losing.

My friends, living life alert, awake, focused, and purposeful is very hard work. It's hard because there is also at work in us a very powerful pull called "entropy." The need to fight against it never ends. Entropy is that powerful pull that does not want us to exert ourselves, that clings to the old and familiar, that is fearful of change and effort, that desires comfort at any cost and the absence of pain at any price. This parable challenges us, "with lamps lit," to stand up to the powerful pull to fall asleep on our feet and to live our lives, consciously, in preparation for meeting Christ at any time.

Throughout my thirty years as a priest I have been aware of the powerful tug of entropy. Fighting it is a major part of the spiritual discipline. I have seen it at work, especially in marriage and in priesthood. I have witnessed the "dozing off" of marriage partners as soon as the honeymoon was over, and the "dozing off" of priests no sooner than the bishop's hands are lifted from their heads! How many times have I run into couples several years after I had married them, only to be shocked by what I saw? How could two handsome people, alive and alert, fit and full of hope, turn into two complaining, overweight, and dispirited people in such a short time? How many times has a marriage partner, on the verge of divorce, told me in counseling, "I had no idea it was coming; I couldn't see it happening"? The other day I was examining the class photos hung in one of the halls at the seminary I attended. Every once in a while I would be caught by particular portraits and find myself asking how so-and-so, a handsome, talented, and energetic seminarian, had turned into such a tired and angry, burned-out and burned-up old cleric in the middle of his life?

My friends, living life awake, alert, focused, and purposeful is hard work. It can be done. It's worth it, but it doesn't happen by accident — it happens by design. Heroic discipline is often required to stay awake! Therefore, let us keep our lamps oiled and burning brightly. Should he happen to come at midnight or before sunrise, in our twenties or in our nineties, and find us prepared, it will go well with us.

RESPONSIBILITY

Let no one look down on you because of your youth. Pay attention to yourself and the work you do. Persevere at both tasks.

I Timothy 4

One of my favorite images of a priest is that of "wounded healer." A priest is a man who uses one of his hands to bandage his own wounds and the other hand to bandage the wounds of others. As a flawed human being, he must tend to his own needs. As a priest, he is called to be of service to others in need. A priest should be both good and good at what he does. The happy, holy, and effective priest is the one who balances looking after himself and looking out for others. There is an old Latin axiom every priest knows: *nemo dat quod non habet*. If you don't have it, you can't give it!

In our first reading today, Paul is writing from prison to his young fellow-missionary, Timothy. Paul is about to be martyred. Timothy is discouraged in his ministry and wants to give up and come home. Paul writes to him to encourage him and to give him a last bit of advice. He tells young Timothy to stand firm, to remain faithful, and to hang in there, even if chaos is swirling all about him. He tells Timothy not to let anyone look down on him because he is young. He tells him to take care of himself and to take care of the ministry he has been given to do. In business, they call it group maintenance and task maintenance. The challenge of every business is to take care of the workers and to produce a good product. They are so interrelated that any business is in peril if its managers do not attend to both.

Robert Bellarmine was a man much like Timothy. He was born during a time when the Catholic Church was corrupt to the core. He could have joined the reformers who left the church, but he chose to stay and do what he could to reform it from the inside. He became a Jesuit at age eighteen. Despite Bellarmine's protest and tears, the Pope made him a cardinal. He worked his whole life to reform the church from the inside. Now we remember him as one of the church's greatest reformers. Saint Robert was a man of balance – he looked after himself and after the work he was called to do. He was faithful to both till the end. He was holy and effective.

Like Timothy who lived in frustrating times, and Robert Bellarmine who lived in religiously corrupt times, we live and work in a world with many problems. Shrill voices bid us go in this direction and that. These voices often seduce us with their convincing rhetoric into making choices that are not good for us or for the people around us. Many of you are away from home for the first time or are beginning to make that break. There will be no one around to make you be good or do well. It will be something that you will have to choose for yourself. Some will be seduced into self-defeating and destructive behaviors. Others, through the grace of God, will follow the advice of St. Paul and be able to stand up to their own cowardice and laziness and do hard things for their own good, growing in the process into more than they could have imagined.

Happy married couples know that to keep their marriage healthy and life-giving, each partner must be dedicated to both individual improvement and to paying attention to their partner's needs, no matter what other married people do or don't do. Happy marriages are possible today for those who have the personal and spiritual discipline to make their vows a reality. It takes two happy and attentive people to make a great marriage.

Teachers and administrators know that they cannot rely solely on what they learned to get their degree; they must continue to learn and grow within their field while they must also dedicate themselves to honing their teaching skills. Without both, a teacher cannot expect to be truly effective. A good teacher is a perpetual student.

Last week, I gave a five day retreat to eighty-three priests from Evansville at Barkley Lake State Park. The theme was "minding your call." I challenged them to take care of themselves and take care of the ministry to which they have been called. I challenged them to be both good and good at it. I challenged them to take responsibility for their own happiness in spite of all the aggravations, pressure, and frustration they may have to face each day. I challenged them to rid themselves of old resentments, excuses, and scapegoats and to bloom where they are planted. I challenged them to look out for each other. Priests need the support and encouragement of each other, especially today when we living out a vocation that is not as popular as it once was! I reminded them that we have no hope of ever attracting young men to the priesthood unless we priests ourselves live happy and effective lives, unless we are both good and good at what we do.

At the beginning of another academic year, knee deep in opportunities to learn and grow, I believe the words of the dying Paul to the young Timothy are appropriate for all of us. They outline a good agenda for the new school year. Let us be mindful and respectful of ourselves, and let us dedicate ourselves to doing well what we have set out to do. Let us heed Paul's advice to the young Timothy:

> *Let no one have contempt for your youth, but set an example for those who believe, in speech, conduct, love, faith, and purity. . . . attend to the reading, exhortation, and teaching. . . . Be diligent in these matters, be absorbed in them, so that your progress may be evident to everyone. Attend to yourself and to your teaching; persevere in both tasks, for by doing so you will save both yourself and those who listen to you.*

PATIENCE

When the crop grew and bore fruit, the weeds appeared as well.

Matthew 13

Most of us in this country, at least compared with the rest of the world, live in an "all-you-can-eat-buffet" society. For six or seven dollars, you can graze among the salads and pile your plate as many times as you want at the Denny's Food Bar. From the looks of some of the bellies the last time I was in there, there are dozens of people who take advantage of this arrangement on a regular basis. There are always a few who seem determined to see just how much they can stack on one plate, as if it might not be there by the time they are ready for a clean plate. Rather than being selective and discerning about what they put into their bodies, the name of the game seems to be eat it all, simply because it's there!

Beyond the "hog trough" approach to feeding our bodies, we live in a society where we can also stuff our minds from the buffet of information that is readily available to us, especially now over the internet. Rather than being selective and discerning about what they put into their minds, for some people the name of the game seems to be take-it-all-in, garbage and all, simply because it's there!

Jesus may not have known about the all-you-can-eat buffet or the anything-goes internet, but he did know that every one of us has a mixture of good and bad, truth and error, in our minds and hearts. He taught his disciples about it in a way they could understand — by means of a parable — a little story packed with wisdom. The good seeds are thoughts in our minds that are in harmony with the indwelling Christ — whatever is good, positive, and constructive. The weed seeds are negative thoughts and beliefs in our minds — whatever is bad, negative, and destructive.

To understand what Jesus has to teach us today about this mixture of good and bad, truth and error, that we are always carrying in our minds and hearts, we must know a few things about the details of this parable. What makes this parable so clever is the **kind** of weeds that were sown among the wheat. The weed mentioned here was called "tares" or "darnel." It was a common for a farmer's enemies to make trouble by sewing these insidious weed seeds in a newly planted wheat field. Why this particular kind of weed? First, when tares sprout, they look almost identical to wheat. Second, as the tares grow, their roots entwine themselves around the roots of the newly sprouted wheat. By the time you realize what has happened, it is too late. You can not pull up one without pulling up the other.

What is a farmer to do? If you go out and start trying to pull out the weeds, you pull up the wheat along with them. The wise farmer must be patient, Jesus says. Even though weeds and wheat are indistinguishable at an early stage, the tares only grow to a certain height. After that, it is easy to tell the difference. When the wheat is ripe and ready for harvest, the farmer cuts off the taller heads of wheat first. Then he cuts the shorter weeds and gathers them into bundles, not only getting rid of the weeds, but gaining some good fuel for cooking and heating in a land short of trees. The patient farmer wins two ways: he has a good crop of wheat, and he uses the weeds to his own advantage.

Parables are not meant to teach us about first century Palestinian agricultural practices. They are meant to teach us about God and our relationship to God. They have to be translated. So what is it that Jesus wants us to know? Several things occurred to me. (1) Jesus wants us to know that every person on earth, every culture on earth, has a mixture of truth and error, good and bad, coexisting at the same time. Yes, God sows good thoughts in our minds and hearts, but evil exists and does its work too, though it is only temporary and is destined to end. (2) Jesus wants us to know that it is good to be enthusiastic about our own spiritual growth and making the world a better place, but he also cautions us not to be over-zealous and impatient. A person can be so intent on rooting out evil that he can end up rooting out much that is good and helpful. Like the wheat and tares in the parable, good and evil are hard to tell apart at the early stages of growth. Patience is needed to allow God to reveal good and evil clearly to us. (3) Sometimes even what appears to be evil and bad can turn out to be useful in the spiritual life. As the parable teaches us, even the bundles of weeds can be used for cooking and heating. (4) When all is said and done, it is God who will purify all that is bad in us. All those false, bad, and counterproductive thoughts that limit our progress and keep us unhappy will be someday be redeemed by the fire of the Spirit. Good and evil will be in constant struggle within us and around us throughout our lives, but at God's great harvest, good will triumph — not so much through our own doing, but through God's patient work in us!

All of us, some time or another, share the sentiments of St. Paul who once wrote about himself, "I end up doing the bad things I want to avoid and avoid doing the good things I really want to do." This parable reminds us to be patient and open ourselves up to God so that God can do his work within us. We are saved, not through our own efforts at goodness, but though God's own saving work. Even if we are discouraged by our own sins and failings and weaknesses, God is not finished with us yet. Even if the goodness in us is as small as a mustard seed or as insignificant as a dab of yeast, in time and with God's help, it will crowd out all the evil tendencies and weaknesses that we have within us. We have God's word on it! So we must be patient with ourselves.

We must be patient with each other, as well. Faced with the sins and weaknesses of others, there is a tendency to be over-zealous in our judgement. History has shown us over and over again that today's sinner may be tomorrow's saint. We must love the sinner, even if we hate the sin. We can not see as God sees. We see externals. Only God sees into the heart. Therefore we must love one another, yes, even our enemies, because even our enemies can be transformed by the loving patience of God.

A final word to the impatient and over-zealous religious fanatics among us: plant your good seeds, but leave the weeding to God! Killing in the name of God is still a fact of life, even in our lifetime: Jews and Arabs, Catholics and Protestants, Hindus and Moslems. Ethnic cleansing, gay bashing, and racist atrocities make the news every night, people killing each other in the belief they are weeding the world for God. This parable has much to teach us, even after all these years. Let those with ears to hear it, hear it!

My friends, every individual is a field of weeds and wheat growing together; every nation and people are a field of weeds and wheat growing together. God has sown good seed everywhere, in the hearts of all his children. Yes, there are weeds within us and within each other. Sometimes, good and bad are hard to distinguish, in fact they look almost alike sometimes. In our zeal to have things neat and orderly, we attack what scares us, both within ourselves and in each other.

We are so tempted to judge! Jesus is the source of good seed. His seed will come to harvest. The weeds may be a nuisance, but they are not the ultimate winners. Good will triumph over evil because God has seen to it. We need to work with God in sowing our minds and hearts with good seed. We must resist the urge to judge and uproot what "appears" to be bad because our eyesight is not all that reliable. God can transform even weeds into something useful. So relax. It's not your job to be the savior of the world. Jesus has already done that! God's will **will** be done on earth as it is in heaven.

ANXIETY

Have no anxiety at all. . . . Keep on doing what you have learned and received and heard and seen in me. Then the God of peace will be with you.

Philippians 4

Have you ever had the experience of being sea-sick? I have, at least three times — once crossing Lake Michigan, once in the Caribbean, and once going to the island of Nantucket; and I will never forget how being seasick feels. As the experience starts everything around me seems to rock, churn, shake, agitate, whip, convulse, swirl, jiggle, and spin. I turn green, break out in a cold sweat and puke my guts out. The only relief I've ever found is to lie flat on my back and hope to die. I have since heard that the best thing you can do when seasickness overtakes you is to focus on something solid and stationary, like a building on the shoreline.

Our second reading today is from St. Paul's letter to the Christians at Philippi, a small community of believers he had established on one of his missionary journeys. The Christians in Philippi were not seasick, but close to it. The little community of believers was churning and rocking and convulsing. They were struggling against attacks from their neighbors for being Christian. They were confused by some visiting missionaries who were teaching things contrary to what Paul had taught them. They were torn apart by bickering and disharmony from within their own ranks. It is to this little group of Christians that Paul says, "Don't lose your cool. Don't let all the chaos get to you! Stay focused on something solid! Keep on doing what you have learned and received and heard and seen in me." If you do that, he says, "the peace of God will be with you," no matter how much crap is swirling around you!

I can understand how those Philippian Christians might have felt in the whirlwind of cultural change. Halfway through my seminary training, the Catholic Church went from being calm and serene and predictable to being stormy and chaotic, almost overnight. We changed, not with a whimper, but with a bang. We wore long black cassocks to class one day and cut-off blue jeans the next. One semester you could be kicked out for drinking a beer on campus; the next semester the monastery got a liquor license and opened a beer and pizza pub in the basement of the gym. We went from celebrating Mass in Latin with the priest facing the wall to celebrating Mass in English with the priest facing the people. Churches changed from a space of hushed whispers to one filled with endless talking and stand-up comedy! Many Catholics got seasick during this tumultuous period. Mass attendance fell from about 90% to 24% in 25 years. People used to look down on you if you didn't go to church. Now people look down on you if you do! Priests, nuns, and religious brothers took off their habits; and thousands of them left their communities to get secular jobs and get married. There were twelve priests ordained in my class in 1970. Five of us are left. People used to admire you if you became a priest or nun. Now they think you're nuts.

When I was ordained in 1970, I knew exactly what I was getting into. I knew I would serve the church as a priest in the eye of a storm. I did it anyway. I did it on purpose. I realized back then that I would be a priest in another one of those many tumultuous periods in church history. I knew, even back then, that I was going to have to learn to ride the waves without puking out my own guts or I would not be any good at helping others weather the storms of change.

To help me remember this fact, I selected a personal theme song and a gospel story to hang onto. The song is an old Quaker Song entitled "How Can I Keep From Singing?" I have played it every year for twenty-nine years on the anniversary of my ordination. The lyrics go like this:

> No storm can shake my inmost calm
> while to that Rock I'm clinging.
> Since love is Lord of heaven and earth,
> how can I keep from singing?
> Through all the tumult and the strife,
> I hear the music ringing.
> It sounds and echoes in my soul;
> how can I keep from singing?

The gospel story I have adopted for myself is the one about St. Peter's walk on water. In a storm one day, Jesus came walking toward the boat that Peter and the apostles were in. Jesus invited Peter to get out of the boat and walk toward him over the water. As long as Peter focused on Jesus, he was able to walk on water. When he looked down at how deep the water was, or looked around at the waves and the wind, he began to sink. That song and that story have helped me weather the storm over the last thirty years. Clinging to the Rock and focusing on Jesus have helped me hang in there. I'm still going. I am happy. I plan to be a priest, no matter how ferocious the storm, until I'm dead, God willing!

I am not unique. I know I am facing a whole group of young people who are also trying to grow up, to find their way, to keep their balance in some storm like a developing relationship or the absence of one, pressures to succeed and make good grades, to be popular, beautiful, thin, and well-off. Some of you have come from families afflicted with divorce, abuse, addictions, and God knows what else. Others may be facing unwanted pregnancies, sexual orientation issues, or some chronic disease. I hope that for most of you life is going well, even great. But for those who need the peace of Christ that St. Paul speaks about to the Philippians, let me share with you how you can have that "inmost calm that no storm can shake."

Personally, I take St. Paul's advice. I focus on something solid. I just "keep on doing what I have learned and received and heard and seen" in the Scriptures. I try to remember that God loves me without condition. It's a free gift. It is always there, no matter what! I also try to remember that God has told us that no matter how many awful things might happen to us and around us, when all is said and done, good will win out; and things will be OK. When I keep returning to that, I can whistle in the dark, sing in the rain, and laugh even when I am in pain. God loves me, I am in good hands, and everything will be OK! That is the rock to which I cling when storms invade my life. When I keep coming back to that, I can feel peaceful inside even in times when everything outside seems to be in chaos.

And, yes, I pray as I go along. One of my favorite prayers for a peaceful center is the one the priest says at every Mass, right after the Lord's Prayer. "Deliver us Lord from every evil and grant us peace in our day. Keep us free from sin and protect us from all anxiety as we wait in joyful hope for the coming of our Savior, Jesus Christ."

I wish all of you peace, especially those going through a personal storm right now. Do not abandon the ship just because you cannot control the waves. Focus on something solid. Take St. Paul's advice to the Christians at Philippi, buffeted by external attacks and internal dissention.

Have no anxiety at all. . . . Keep on doing what you have learned and received and heard and seen in me. Then the God of peace will be with you.

RENEWAL

. . . people were astonished at his teaching. . .

Mark 1

We're up to our ears in "new beginnings." It's so bad that if I hear the phrase "new millennium" one more time, I believe I will scream! But here we are in our Scripture reading cycle at the *beginning* of the Gospel of Mark, where we are presented with the *beginnings* of Jesus ministry. Mark is the first gospel to have been written down, and it is the shortest. Mark wastes no time. He races from one thing to the next to tell his story, as if a clock were ticking and a decision needed to be made before time runs out. In the space of only one chapter, Jesus recognizes God's call to action while listening to John preach, receives God's approval and grace for the task at hand at his baptism, reviews his options for action in the desert, and chooses his disciples.

Still in chapter one, tonight's reading describes Jesus in the pulpit of the Capernaum synagogue. Scholars believe that Capernaum was where Jesus chose to make his home after leaving his boyhood home of Nazareth. It is from the Capernaum synagogue pulpit that Jesus launches his public ministry. It was customary in those days for the synagogue leader to call on anyone in the congregation to read the scriptures and give a sermon. As soon as Jesus took the pulpit, his audience knew that they were hearing something new, something refreshing, something more appealing, something that rang with truth. His words were a breath of fresh air, a change from the old, stale, repetitious, and droning legalisms that had been coming from the lips of an endless stream of rabbis for as long as they could remember. They sat up and paid attention. Because his preaching was so compelling, the congregation was left spellbound.

Jesus "did not come to destroy the law and the prophets." He came, not to abandon the old time religion or to start a whole new religion, but to renew the old religion and to restore its "soul.". In Jesus' day, the old time religion had lost its soul, lost its punch, lost its ability to energize people. It had become so fat, so tedious, so top-heavy and so overly complicated that it was driving people away from God, instead of drawing them closer to God.

In a way, much religion today has lost its soul, lost its punch, lost its ability to energize peoples' faith. In many places today, religion has again become so tired and tedious that it is driving people away from God, rather than bringing them to God. The last statistics I have read said that 90% of Americans believe in God, but only 19 % attend church on a regular basis. Many more are individualistic spiritual seekers in the "new age movement," going it alone, without the guidance or help of a long-standing faith group. Presbyterians, Catholics, Episcopalians, and Lutherans face a critical priest or minister shortage. Hundreds of Roman Catholics have left our Louisville parishes and joined the local mega-church, Southeast Christian, at least for now!

Yes, organized religion needs a breath of fresh air today, like the fresh air that Jesus brought to the pulpit of the Capernaum synagogue. But the question is: who is going to do it if everybody simply says, "hey, this doesn't serve me, my needs are not being met" and walks away from the church! When I was ordained in 1970, priests were leaving the priesthood like never before; Mass attendance had begun to plummet. Of the twelve priests ordained with me, only five of us are left! I remember making a decision then, a decision that I have made over and over again ever since, a decision not to do what most people did. I decided that I was going to stay and try to be part of that breath of fresh air, to do what I could to renew the church from the inside out!

Over my last thirty years as a priest, I have come to the conclusion that many Catholics crave a vibrant, life-giving church; but they are waiting for someone else to provide it for them! Because they are not part of the solution, they are part of perpetuating the problem. There can never be a strong church when all its members are weak or disengaged.

So, to bring today's message home, I ask you, "Are you willing to renew yourself spiritually so that when enough of us have done that, we will wake up some morning and notice that the church has been renewed?" When I teach preaching to our seminarians, I often remind them that they will never be able to do group spiritual direction from the pulpit without being on a serious spiritual journey themselves. As in many other areas, in preaching, if you don't have it, you can't give it! The church will never be a well of spiritual energy unless its members exude spiritual energy.

I am more and more convinced that the church will never

be renewed through an adolescent search for some kind of magical structural change. If we are to be renewed as a church, it will only be "one heart at a time." You don't have to sign up for anything. You don't have to attend meetings. All you have to do is to commit to your own spiritual growth and let this weekly Eucharist nourish you — let yourself be nourished by God and nourished by us who gather with you to do the same. When enough of us do that, we will feed each other spiritually, and we will attract, by word of mouth, other people who are spiritually hungry! We might even fill that new chapel when they get it done!

SURRENDER

Unless a grain of wheat falls to the ground and dies, it remains just a grain of wheat; but if it dies, it produces much fruit.

John 12

I heard a story years ago about how native peoples capture monkeys. They take a hollowed out gourd and fill it with peanuts. Before nailing it to a tree, they cut a small hole in the gourd, just big enough for a monkey to stick his hand into. When the monkeys grab a peanut, they cannot pull their hands out of the gourd. Instead of letting go of the peanut, they hold onto it and howl till their captors come and take them away. People are like that sometimes. They hang onto relationships long after they are over. They hang onto old grudges for years after the slight. They hang onto dead-end routines until their lives are a bore. They hang on to parents, spouses, and kids long after they are gone. They howl in pain until their lives are crippled. All they would have to do is to "let go," to let go of the peanut so to speak, but they can't bring themselves to do it and so perpetuate their own suffering

Jesus spoke often of the process of "letting go." In today's gospel, instead of monkeys and peanuts, Jesus uses the agricultural image of a sprouting grain of wheat. Unless a tiny grain of wheat gives up its life as a single grain of wheat and is buried in the earth, it stays just a grain of wheat. But if it is planted in the ground, it disintegrates as a single grain of wheat so that eventually it can sends up a shoot that produces fifty times as many grains of wheat. The point? When we "let go" of one way of being ourselves, we allow ourselves to experience yet better ways of being ourselves.

God sent his own Son into the world to teach us this lesson in a dramatic "show and tell" sort of way! As the Son of God, Jesus was totally committed to offering himself up to his Father. Over and over again, he completely let go of his own will and did God's will instead. He let go of fame, family, fortune, possessions, power, and finally even let go of his very life on a bloody cross — so that we may have a full life! "While we were still sinners, Christ died for us!" Because of his fidelity, because he trusted God so completely, God raised him up on that first Easter morning. He now lives in us, his followers, and invites us to do the same: to let go and let God as a way of life! Jesus has promised us, his followers, that after we have triumphed over a million little deaths in this life, we will triumph even over our final deaths, rising to new life with Him for all eternity!

Letting go and letting God is not to be confused with being passive. Letting go and letting God, dying and rising as a way of life, is anything but passive! It is, rather, radical engagement with life itself! It is intentional living, in contrast to unconscious living. Each of us guards a gate of change that can only be unlocked from the inside. When we recognize and accept that something in ourselves may have to die, we become frightened. We tend, naturally, to resist change and to hang onto the familiar, even if it is slowly killing us. The ego, that collection of qualms and convictions, dreads its own demise. At some point, we have to decide just how much we want to change. Choosing to let go, choosing to die to our old self so that we may rise to a new self, is a kind of suicide. We don't have to change. We have the ability to filter reality to suit our level of courage. But in the end, if we choose to hang on to the peanut, we die; when we choose to let go of it, we live!

I have been trying for several years now to intentionally live a life of "death and resurrection," letting go of one self to become another. I know from experience that the grain of wheat dying to become a bunch of grains of wheat is absolutely true, both on a physical, as well as a spiritual level. I'm not holding myself up as a master at it, but let me give you two example from my own life where it has worked for me. (1) I used to be very, very bashful. Being around people was painful, but having to perform in front of people was agony. I never read in front of my classmates when I was in the seminary. I gave one four minute homily before I was ordained. The main role of a priest is to preach, and there I was, shaking in my boots and avoiding every opportunity to be in front of people! Before I could get over it, I had to be willing to let "the old me" die! I faced my fear. I stood up to my own resistance. It was a long and painful death. But a "new me" was gradually born — the one that has traveled all over the country giving homilies and speeches in front of thousands of strangers at least once a week. I even teach preaching at my old seminary once in a while! (2) As I have mentioned before, I was distant from my father for the first part of my life. He was a verbally abusive rage-aholic. In my mid-thirties, I was filled with resentment toward him. It was so intense that it was crippling. It tainted everything I touched, and it possessed my mind like an ever-present demon. I was sick and tired of being angry, and I resented my own obsessive thinking about it. I decided to let that resentful and angry me die. I decided to let go of it. I decided to forgive without condition. It was not quick or easy. It was the most difficult thing I have ever done in my life. But I did it. The "new me" sees him now with the eyes of compassion. I give him credit for doing the best he knew how, the best he could, even though it was not what I needed. I had to admit that taking offense is just as sinful as giving offense. I do not miss that angry and resentful old me. For my own sake, I'm glad God helped me to forgive. "Unless a grain of wheat dies, it remains just a grain of wheat, but if it dies, it produces much fruit."

Any examples from your life? What is holding you back from a richer, happier, and more fulfilling life? Is it an old grudge you just won't let go of? Is it bitterness over an old relationship gone bad? Is it fear and cowardice in face of the unknown? Is it an untrue and distorted self-image that has resulted from past hurts and traumas? "Unless the grain of wheat dies, it remains just a grain of wheat, but if it dies, it produces much fruit." Let go of the peanut and live! Hold onto it and die!

Yes, it's true in a millions ways! "Unless a grain of wheat falls to the ground and dies, it remains just a grain of wheat; but if it dies, it produces much fruit." If we become that grain of wheat over and over again in this life, if we intentionally engage life itself, then we have the chance of going where we never dreamed of going, a chance of reaching a level of happiness we have never imagined. If not, we need to know that we are stuck because we choose to be stuck, simply because we are lazy cowards in the face of change. Finally, after dying a million little deaths so that we may live, we can be that grain of wheat in face of our own deaths, willing finally to let our earthly lives go, so as to open ourselves to sharing eternal life with Jesus himself!

GLIMPSES

Peter said to Jesus, "Master, it is good that we are here; let us make three tents, one for you, one for Moses, and one for Elijah." But he did not know what he was saying.

Luke 9

Voices from heaven! People from the past! Brilliant clothes! Approaching death! I cannot read this story without thinking about my mother. She died in 1976 of breast cancer. A few days before she died, she sat up and pointed to the end of her bed. She said she could see angels in brilliant purple robes. Later she began speaking to her dead brothers and sisters who, she told us, were standing around her bed. She saw just the ones who had died, not her living brothers and sisters. Cynics might dismiss this as hallucinations or the power of suggestion. But at that point she no longer needed pain killers because her cancer had spread to her brain, and for some reason she was pain-free, but conscious. Besides, this happened several years before the first book came out about near-death experiences. I don't know for sure what was really going on, but I do not think it is too far fetched to believe that God gave her a "taste of heaven" or a "glimpse of glory" to sustain her in her final hours. Besides, there is an ancient funeral prayer I have said many, many times. "May the angels lead you into Paradise. May the martyrs come to welcome you and take you to the holy city, the new and eternal Jerusalem. May choirs of angels welcome you and lead you to the bosom of Abraham; and where Lazarus is poor no longer, may you find eternal rest." She died peacefully, without a struggle.

Voices from heaven! People from the past! Brilliant clothes! Approaching death!

Last week Jesus went to the desert to pray. This week he goes up on a mountain to pray. Knowing his death is imminent, Jesus invites his closest companions to a little mountaintop retreat to prepare them for the trials ahead. While they are at prayer, Jesus becomes radiant. His white robes take on an unnatural glow, as they will in the resurrection story later on. He converses with the ancient prophets of long ago. The disciples get a "glimpse of the glory to come." This "preview," "foretaste," "sneak preview," "glimpse of glory" would sustain them during the dark hours to come, the rough road ahead.

Darkness, loss, setbacks, suffering, doubt, and lack of faith are part of every spiritual journey. God's promises always come true, but waiting for them to come true often takes nerves of steel and the patience of Job. As in the mountaintop experience we just read, God often provides special "peak experiences" to sustain us and keep us going during the dark times. These experiences can happen on a retreat, while reading a great book, during times of intense prayer, when we meet special people, or simply in some quiet moment. They may be lightening flashes of insight that don't last long or a spiritual high that lasts for days, but they stay with us for years to come. Remembering them keeps us going during the rough times. My own mother did not want to die. She wanted to live. But after her "glimpse of glory," her "sneak preview of the future," she told me that she was no longer afraid. What she saw sustained her in her last hours. Martin Luther King, Jr., the great gospel preacher and social liberator, must have received one of these "glimpses of glory" toward the end of his life. In his last speech, the day before he was killed, he spoke these words: "We've got some difficult days ahead. But it doesn't matter to me now, because I've been to the mountaintop . . . and I've looked over. And I've seen the promised land. I may not get there with you. But I want you to know tonight that we as a people will get to the promised land. And I'm happy tonight, I'm not worried about anything. I'm not fearing any man. Mine eyes have seen the glory of the coming of the Lord." Many of the great saints of the church "got by" and "hung on" because they were given these "glimpses of glory" and "sneak previews" of what God had in store for them! They were sustained in their great trials by these intense "peak experiences."

The only problem with these "peak experiences," these "moments of grace," is that we try to hang onto them and make them permanent. We want to "make it last" and "preserve" the moment. Peter was bowled over by his religious "high." He wanted to live that "high" for the rest of his life. "Lord, let us put up three tents and stay here forever." "Let's freeze this moment and make this permanent."

That's not what those experiences are for. They are to help us maintain our focus during the harsh realities of life, not to be an alternative to reality. Sustained by what they had seen and what they had experienced, Jesus lead his disciples down the mountain to face the reality of his own death.

I believe that only those who have had one of these experiences can survive and thrive in the church. The church is not perfect. It is always in need of reform. Unless we were able to focus on something beyond the problems, we could not tolerate the messiness of reality. Often people ask me why I want to be a priest, as if it is a big waste of one's life. I know about the problems and the shortcomings of the church, but I have also had some incredible, powerful "peak experiences" in the church. Many times I have felt the very presence of God in the church. It is because of those experiences that I remain in the church and love her dearly. Masses are like that for me. Sometimes Masses seem so dry: the congregation so lifeless and unengaged, the readings strange and confusing, the music depressing, and the homily boring. But if you have ever experienced one Mass that moved you to prayer, made you feel the presence of God, you know that that experience can sustain you during hundreds of Masses that may not be so engaging. My hunch is that the people who remain in the church are those who have had at least one of these powerful experiences. To others, the church appears to be just another religious organization. It is impossible to explain these experiences to those who have not had one of them.

I have spoken before about my long and painful twelve-year journey to priesthood. I really wanted to be a priest, but holding on to that dream was very difficult. Looking back, I realize that I was given little bits and pieces of hope, powerful "peak experiences," as I went along — enough to keep me going. To paraphrase the words of an old Quaker hymn that I love so much; through all the tumult and the strife, I could hear a real, though far-off hymn, that sounded and echoed in my soul. I asked for help and I got it. As a priest for almost thirty years now, I can remember many "peak moments" and "moments of grace" that have helped me do what I have done.

I would like to end this homily by quoting one of my favorite prayers about holding on and hanging in there. The priest says it at every Mass, right after the Lord's Prayer:

> Deliver us, Lord, from every evil and grant us peace in our day. In your mercy keep us free from sin and protect us from all anxiety as we wait in joyful hope for the coming of our Savior, Jesus Christ!

FOUNDATION

"And so I say to you, you are Peter, and upon this rock I will build my church. "

Matthew 16

As a priest for almost thirty years, I have always taken great comfort in the number of complete idiots who have made it to sainthood. Contrary to what most people think, God seems to have a propensity for choosing idiots, thieves, prostitutes, adulterers, bigamists, the handicapped, and the incompetent for his most important assignments. Scripture says "he chooses the weak and makes them strong" and that "God chooses the stone rejected by the builders to become the cornerstone."

I can resonate! When I was in the second grade, I told my beloved teacher Sister Mary Ancilla that I wanted to be a priest. Sister was also in charge of the altar boys. Barely after I told her about wanting to be a priest, I proceeded to flunk the altar boy test — not once, not twice, but three times. This caused Sister to throw up her hands and prophesy: "Ronnie, you're a good kid, but I don't think you'll ever be any good around the altar!" I came within a hair of being kicked out of the seminary during my second year. I was called into the office by the rector, who got up in my face and shouted, "Young man, we're sending you home in the morning. You are a hopeless case!" Miraculously, he gave me another chance. His last words to me, six years later, were these. "Knott, I'm glad you're graduating! You've been a ball and chain around my leg for six years!" This was the head of the seminary speaking! It didn't stop, even after ordination. I was at a reception two weeks after the big event when a middle-aged woman came up to me and asked how many years I had been in school. When I told her twenty years, she gasped and said, "My God, you could have been something!"

Yes, I have taken great comfort from all the idiots and rejects who have gone before me. Abraham and Sarah were so old when they were called that each of them practically had one foot in the grave. Moses had a speech impediment. David was an adulterer and an assassin. Jeremiah whined a lot. Jonah tried to skip town to get away from God. The apostle Simon was a middle eastern terrorist. James and John were politically ambitious "Mama's boys." Mary Magdalene was possessed by demons. Paul and Barnabas fell out and couldn't work together. Paul was an accomplice in the murder of several Christians. Augustine practically had a doctorate in fornication! Thomas Aquinas was extremely overweight and was nicknamed "dumb ox."

The list is endless. but St. Peter, head apostle, takes the cake. His real name was Simon, son of John. Jesus gave him the name *Peteros*, from the word meaning "rock." It was a nickname. Translated into English, his nickname was more like "Rocky." We are told in today's gospel that it was on this "rock" that Jesus built his church. Jesus surely had to hold back a laugh when he picked this name for this man. It had to be said tongue-in-cheek! Simon was anything but solid like a rock. "Sandy" (as in quicksand) would have been more like it!

In reality, Peter was more like a big-hearted klutz who wanted to do the right thing, but just couldn't manage to pull it off. He was forever sticking his foot in his mouth, over-compensating for the last blunder he had made, and having to eat his own words. Some examples might be appropriate here. In today's gospel story, Jesus calls Simon a rock. In next week's story Jesus will call him a satan. Jesus predicts his impending death and the scattering of his disciples; in response good old Peter rushes in, bragging publicly: "Even if everyone else leaves you Lord, you can always depend on me!" A few days later when Jesus was under arrest, it was this same Peter who said, "Jesus, who? I don't think I've ever heard of the man." It was Peter, once again going all out to impress Jesus with his generosity, and trying to be twice as good as everybody else, who suggested that he would be willing to forgive **seven** times. Expecting Jesus to pat him on the back and say, "My, Saint Peter, how wonderful you are!" what Peter instead heard was: "No, Peter not seven times. You must forgive **seventy** times seven times." When Jesus was being arrested in the Garden of Gethsemane, good old Peter lunged forward, sword drawn, to save the day. He swung and (of course) missed, cutting off the ear of one of the servants. After the resurrection, Peter was back in his boat when Jesus appeared, walking on water. The gospel says that Peter was stripped to the waist for fishing. He got so excited the he **put on his coat** and jumped into the water! In another post-resurrection story, Jesus appeared on the shore where a fire had been prepared so breakfast could be cooked early one morning. When Jesus asked his disciples to bring a few of the fish they had just caught, Peter, anxious to make up for past mistakes, rushed forward to dump one hundred fifty-three fish at the feet of Jesus. Good old Rocky!

Many people today are scandalized by the fact that the church, people like me and you, is filled with imperfection. It seems that every week brings another scandal or defection in our church, or in others. I've heard people say, "Why believe any more? The church is full of hypocrites. They have let us down so much. Why bother?"

The first reason to keep believing is this; the validity of this message does not depend upon the personal goodness of the messenger. Church people are only mediums, conduits, and messengers. You need to know that our faith is not in them. We are not the treasure.

Next, people of faith who fail miserably are in need of great compassion. When I go down any list of the names of those who have fallen, one thing is obvious. All those who have fallen have done good work in their lifetimes. They have given many years of dedicated service to the church. Most have done a world of good in some very difficult situations. Now they are forced to live with their own punishment in a world in which, probably, they will be remembered for their weakest moment, not their great moments. Acting with compassion is not the same thing as feeling pity or giving approval. Compassion comes from two words meaning "to suffer with." There, but for the grace of God, go you or I.

Third, the church is not just its leaders. The church is a

community of believers, empowered by Christ to carry on his ministry — however imperfectly. In other words, this is it! Jesus reminded us that we are like a field of weeds and wheat growing together. We are like a dragnet thrown into the sea which collects all kinds of things. We are that wedding reception to which the good and bad alike are invited. We may like to think that Jesus should have known better than to build his church on such weak human beings, but the fact is that Jesus did know what he was doing and he did it anyway. For that reason I think that Peter the Apostle could be our hero at this time in our history, a time of great sifting and sorting, scandals and defections. When many of Jesus' followers drifted away after his teaching on the Bread of Life, they said: "This is hard to take. Who can believe it?" I have always imagined Peter standing there, doubtful and hurt, when Jesus finally turns to him and says, "Peter, will you go away also?" Almost pathetically, torn between confusion and commitment, Peter responds: "I don't understand all of this, Lord. But where else can we go? You have the words of everlasting life."

Fourth, Jesus promises that no matter how weak we may be as individuals, the power of hell will not prevail against us as a community of faith. It's interesting that Jesus made this promise to disciples like Peter, of all people. It's obvious that Jesus prepared the church not only for the pressure of the attacks to come from the outside, but also for the pressure of infidelity that would come from the inside. Yes, we've been through better times — but if you know your church history, you also know we have been through worse times. Yet somehow the Gospel has been handed from one generation to another, unbroken. It may be battered and bruised sometimes, but it gets through. And it will continue to get through because of, and in spite of, this collection of weak human beings that we call the church. Hell can't stop us because God is with us.

We now gather around the table of the Lord to be forgiven for our mistakes and to be strengthened on the Eucharist, our Bread for the journey, our strength for the trip — on the Body and Blood of Jesus Himself.

PROPHETS

John wore clothing made of camel's hair and had a leather belt around his waist. His food was locusts and wild honey.

Matthew 3

Even though he has grown on me over the years, I never liked John the Baptist all that much. Grown men who wear fur coats, eat bugs, and scream a lot make me very, very nervous. This fiery street preacher is way too intense for me! But he had a beard, so I guess he can't be all that bad!

On this, the second Sunday of Advent, the church presents John the Baptist to us for our consideration. No, John the Baptist is not the founder of the Southern Baptist Convention. He was the last in a long line of biblical prophets leading up to the coming of Jesus Christ!

What's a prophet? Influenced by the current explosion of interest in psychics, mediums, fortune tellers, and horoscopes, most people think prophets are people who predict the future! While it is true that, on rare occasions, prophets tell people what will happen in the future, for the **most** part they are people who tell others what is happening right under their very noses. They are more people of insight than foresight. Prophets help people see what is happening in the present, often pointing out things others would rather not see. Prophets are really those people in our midst who rub our noses in the truth, whether we want to see it or not! They are like an external conscience. They rock the boat. They stir up the dust. They make trouble. They disturb sleeping dogs. They will not let individuals or groups doze off or get comfortable. Because prophets are people who make us look at truths we would rather not see, most prophets end up getting themselves killed. Prophets are killed not because they lie about things, but because they tell the truth to people who don't really want to hear the truth.

John the Baptist was such a man. He had insight, and he told the truth. John is known primarily for pointing out the presence of God in the person of Jesus. All the crowds saw when they looked at Jesus was just another young Jewish spiritual seeker from Nazareth. What John saw was God's Son, so he pointed it out to the crowds. John confronted King Herod with his own wrongdoing. John had the nerve to get up in the king's face and tell him, "Herod, the way you are now living is wrong, flat out wrong! You're living with your brother's wife!" That's what prophets do — they are tacky enough to name sin when they see it, letting the chips fall where they may! John the Baptist was beheaded for his comments, not because he lied about the king, not because he tried to have him overthrown, but because he told the truth to a man who didn't want to hear spoken aloud what his conscience had already told him.

Because the truth often hurts and we want to avoid the pain, God sends prophets into our midst to call us back to the truth, to remind us of what we already know, but don't want to admit. Because we have this human ability to lie to ourselves and to fall for the lies of others, even to the point of numbing our own consciences, God sends truth-telling prophets who hold us to our own principles. Prophets are sent to expose lies, both those lies we tell ourselves and those we conspire with others to tell. Because we want to do what we want to do, we beat, silence, jail, excommunicate, shun, exile, and even murder the voices of those who dare challenge us. We murder the messenger because we don't want to hear the message.

My friends, think about it! The people who make us the angriest are not those who lie about us, but the people who tell the truth about us! It is good to remind ourselves once in a while that people who tell us what we want to hear are not necessarily our friends, just as people who tell us things we don't want to hear are not necessarily our enemies. Sometimes it is those who love us most who challenge our behaviors. Sometimes it is those who love us least who ignore, maybe even encourage us in our bad behaviors. Jesus said that "the truth will make us free." He might have said, "the truth will make you free, but first it will aggravate the hell out of you." Yes, the truth often hurts. We have all heard the expression "the painful truth." That's why we try so hard to find a way around it; we want to avoid the pain or the work it will take to change. For our own good and the good of our communities, Gods sends prophets to challenge us and to remind us of the truth, even when we are lying through our teeth either to ourselves or to the people around us!

Who are the prophets of today? They are many. Some of them have been murdered or jailed in our lifetimes. Martin Luther King was shot for rubbing this country's nose in the injustice of racism. Pope John Paul II stood up to the evils of communism in eastern Europe. Mother Theresa reminded the world of the dignity and worth of the helpless, diseased, and forgotten. Bishop Oscar Romero of El Salvador stood up for the poor of Central America and was shot to death at the altar while saying Mass. Nelson Mandela was imprisoned for years for standing up to the evils of apartheid in South Africa. There are those fighting for the rights of women, against the evils of capital punishment, fighting the tragedy of homelessness, the scandal of mass abortions, the sin of child abuse, and on and on. Yes, God continues to send prophets to wake us up, especially when our consciences have shut down! Maybe sitting in front of me tonight are a few prophets of the future, sent by God to rub our noses in truths that we would just as soon not see!

CLEANSED

Jesus made a whip out of cords. He drove out those sell-
ing sheep, doves and oxen, spilled the coins of the money
changers and overturned their tables.

John 2

There is nothing quite as exciting as a downtown church. Downtown churches are quite often magnets for kooks! Our Cathedral, downtown at Fifth and Mohammed Ali, is one of those churches. I was pastor there from 1983-1997. My first day there, one of the street people decided to take his clothes off and run around the cathedral, naked! You can imagine what it did to the little old ladies who like to quietly pray there throughout the day! Another week day, just as I was about to come out of the sacristy for the noon Mass, I noticed a drunk passed out in the bishop's chair! I still regret not running to get my camera! One Sunday, a crazy man with a knife threatened to kill one of us priests over a sermon he didn't like. A policeman and I had to wrestle him down between the pews, handcuff him, and take him out! The same man used to carry a big sign up and down the sidewalk in front of the cathedral which said"Welcome to the church of Satan! Pastor approves sexual perversion." I was that pastor and we welcomed gays and lesbians, as well as other hurt and marginalized Catholics. On another Sunday, a crazed woman decided to run up to the altar, right in the middle of Mass, and start screaming from the Book of Revelations. I carefully led her down the aisle to the back. The church was full. Just as we got two-thirds of the way down the aisle, she screamed, "Get behind me Satan! Jesus is coming soon!" Three times in one week, we had to clean the face of a statue of Mary holding the dead Jesus. Someone was sticking hands full of **used** toilet paper right on her face! I could go on for an hour! Yes, downtown churches in any big city can be exciting places to work!

The Temple in Jerusalem was such a place, except much, much bigger. It attracted all kinds of people from all over, especially during the great Feast of Passover. The Temple precincts were literally crammed with people because every adult male Jew who lived within fifteen miles was required by law to attend the Passover Feast and possibly offer a sacrifice. Besides those who had to go, there were others who came from every part of the known world at that time. It was the dream of very Jew to go to the Temple in Jerusalem at least once in his or her lifetime. One commentator says that, as astonishing as it sounds, it is likely that as many as two and a quarter million people sometimes gathered in Jerusalem to keep the Passover. Imagine entering the Temple area packed elbow to elbow with people, wading through a sea of sheep and oxen dung, stalls selling animals for sacrifice, and hawkers yelling the best exchange rate from a bevy of money changers tables. Why money changers? People normally used Greek or Roman coins, but since they had pagan graven images on them, they could not be used in the Temple, they had to be exchanged! It was literal "money laundering." All this created a great market-like atmosphere of noise and odors, pushing and shoving, buying and selling, grabbing and snatching, all in the name of religion!

At the great Feast of Passover, this scene must have shaken the religious sensitivity of Jesus to the core! Jesus cracking a home-made whip, kicking over tables, freeing pigeons and doves into the air, stampeding cattle and sheep, and people running to get out of the way, must have been a sight to see! What caused Jesus to lose his cool when he came into the Temple precincts that Passover Eve? First of all, on arrival, everybody was required to pay a temple tax, equivalent to two days wages. But they didn't take American Express! They had to get it changed into "acceptable money" so besides having to come up with two days wages, they also had to pay an exorbitant fee for changing their money into acceptable money. Secondly, people who wished to offer an animal for sacrifice had to bring an unblemished one. To be sure the animals were acceptable, people had to get their animal inspected by inspectors. There was a fee for that! More often than not, home-grown animals were rejected. Of course, there were already inspected animals available for a price, a huge inflated price. It was bare-faced blackmail for money, all in the name of religion. It was this exploitation of people, simple people who wanted to get close to God, that moved Jesus to flaming anger. The heart of Jesus ached when he saw poor people, wanting desperately to please God and do the right thing, being taken advantage of. They just wanted to feel the presence of God, and they were being outrageously abused and used. A place of prayer had become a marketplace. People of prayer had become pawns in the hand of a religious system gone amuck! What started out to be a good thing had gradually turned into a religious nightmare! Religions have a business side, but when religion becomes a business, watch out! It was time to clean house, and Jesus knew it!

Religion always has two sides: the exoteric and the esoteric, the container and the contents, what happens inside the heart and what happens outside in the tangible world. Christianity is an inner path and a world religion. Over and over again in history, the church has had to be dragged through reformations after the packaging had become overly important to the detriment of the contents. Humans have a knack for making the trivial important and making the important trivial! Vatican Council II said the church is *semper reformanda*, always in need of reform! In this special year, set aside for intense self-examination, the Pope has been apologizing to almost everybody for the sins of our past, for the times we have turned "our Father's house into a marketplace" in several different ways. Lent is needed because, once in a while, we all need to stop and clean house!

It's easy to read today's gospel and be enraged about "those awful religious authorities" back then! Real easy! It's easy to identify and villify money hungry TV evangelists! Real easy! The message when we do that is: we're better than they are! What we are challenged to do is to look within ourselves, not to look at others. How often have we been guilty of the same dynamics? We could ask ourselves these questions. Do I use people? Do I take advantage of other people? Am I always trying to work the system, shaving the truth, and getting more than I give? How much have I given in to the idolatry of materialism? In what parts of my life am

I kidding myself? There is a part of all of us that is always pulling our attention away from what is truly important. It must be recognized, named, and stood up to! There is a part of us that is always choosing the easy way, cutting corners, and living out a life centered on self. Lent is about a house cleaning of the heart. We are asked to take a good look at what's going on with us, then to overturn and drive out all that doesn't count and to refocus on what really counts. Lent is about giving up the spiritual trash in our hearts, not candy bars and beer! Jesus cleansed the temple today. Lent is a time to cleanse the temple of our hearts!

VIGILANCE

Be watchful! Be alert! Watch, therefore! What I say to you, I say to all: 'Watch!'

Mark 13

I am the second oldest of seven children. As the oldest son I found myself in positions of authority even during childhood. Today's readings reminded me of one occasion when I was put in charge. My mother had to come up here, from Meade County to Louisville, for a hysterectomy. It meant that the seven of us would be left at home most of the day while my father was working. I was put in charge. It was my plan to impress my mother by having a tidy house and a delicious meal on the table the day my mother came home from the hospital. Every day for several days, I marshaled the house-cleaning troops and cooked a wonderful meal, only to be disappointed that she was going to stay "one more day" at the hospital. After several days of false alarms, I was tired of cleaning and cooking. I decided to wait until I was sure she was coming home before I started doing all that work. Guess what? With our guard down, she showed up on a day we least expected. The house was a mess, and there was nothing on the table the day she pulled into the driveway!

Today, we begin the "advent season," a time when the church concentrates on "waiting in joyful hope for the coming of our Savior, Jesus Christ." We wait in three ways: we wait for the annual celebration of Christmas; we wait for the continual coming of Christ, by faith, into the lives of believers; we wait for the day when Christ will come again at the end of time. During the advent season, the image of driving a car comes to mind. To drive successfully, one has to look **backward** into the rear view mirror, one has to look **around** to see what is going on inside the car, and one has to look **forward** out the windshield to see what is coming. So advent is a time to look at the past, the present and the future. "Christ has died! Christ is risen! Christ will come again!"

Advent, then, is **supposed** to be a time of quiet reflectiveness, a time to go inside oneself, a time to slow down and think, a time to remember, take notice and dream. In reality, advent doesn't have a chance in hell! For the next four weeks, we will all be swept up into the opposite: a time of confusion and noise, a time of externalism and materialism, a time of to rush and hurry, a time of waste and excess. Every year I am confronted with a choice − since I can't beat it, do I join it? How do I make advent a retreat in preparation for Christmas, when everyone else around me starts celebrating Christmas the day after Thanksgiving? Why would I put up a tree on Christmas Eve, when everyone else is about to take theirs down? How can I play the longing tunes of advent music when everywhere I go "Joy to the World" blares from every grocery store PA system, car radio, and shopping center lobby? How can I get up enough strength to fight off the church decorating committee who wants to put up the Christmas tree for the second Sunday of Advent so that they can "get it over with?" My brothers and sisters gave up gift-giving years ago. My decorating gets simpler every year, and I do carve out a few hours to be alone. However, celebrating advent as a time of reflection is almost a hopeless cause, a losing battle of swimming against a powerful stream!

I don't think we can persuade the commercial Christmas machine to "cease and desist," to stop the madness in order to celebrate Advent, but maybe there is **something** we can do to preserve **some** of the beauty of this advent season. Maybe we can't "stop, look, and listen" for four weeks, but surely we can build in a few moments here and there to consider our spiritual priorities, even in the rush and madness of another American, commercial, Christmas frenzy.

But don't expect to be admired should you try to buck the system! For many years now, sensing that advent escaped me yet once again, I have turned to New Year's Eve. I have a custom of **not** accepting invitations to New Year's Eve parties. I like to spend the whole evening home, alone, a time all by myself. I love it! I dare not tell those inviting me that I will be home alone, lest they give me that "you must be mentally ill" look. I simply tell them that I already have plans and leave it at that, hoping they will not probe into the exact nature of those plans, thereby forcing me to defend myself at a mental inquest! It is sort of my solution to being deprived of a real advent! Maybe I'm not crazy after all, just a man ahead of his time! The November 29th *Time* magazine cover this year has these headlines, "The Simple New Year's

Eve: Why we're saying no to the hype and opting for a quiet, meaningful evening." I will again this year spend New Year's Eve alone with God, popular or not! And I will love it, yet again!

I'm not here to sell my idea of a good Christmas or New Year's celebration. I am here to sell the idea of celebrating Advent, even a few moments of Advent — taking at least a little time to "stop, look, and listen," to "look back, look around, and look forward," taking time to spend a few moments with your God!

WAITING

Rejoice always. Pray without ceasing. Give thanks constantly.

I Thessalonians

The teachings of Jesus were originally passed from one believer to another by word of mouth, from memory. It took many years before this material was written down in what we call the "books" of the New Testament. The very first one to be written down, about twenty years after Jesus' death, was not one of the gospels, but the First Letter of Paul to the Thessalonians, our second reading tonight. Paul believed that Jesus was going to come back in his lifetime. In this letter he tells the people to prepare themselves for the second coming. Many people took his advice literally. They quit their jobs, sat down and waited. As time went by, he had to write a second letter, the Second Letter to the Thessalonians, to tell them to get up, get back to work, because the exact time was not known. Ever since that time almost 2000 years ago, there have been groups of Christians who have believed that they could comb the scriptures, read the signs, and predict the "second coming." They have usually been dissident groups within Christianity. There were the Gnostics and Montanists in the second century and the Priscillians of fourth century Spain. This thinking appeared again in Europe right before the turn of the last millennium. It appeared again in the thirteenth and fourteenth centuries, again after the Protestant Reformation in Germany and Switzerland, again in eighteenth century Pietism, again in nineteenth century America among sects such as the Jehovah's Witnesses and Seventh Day Adventists. It survives today among many Evangelical and Pentecostal groups, who are in high gear as we enter the third millennium.

What is the Catholic belief about the "second coming?" The Catholic Church teaches that, indeed, Jesus will return, but that no one can predict the time. Even Jesus says in the gospels, "Many will come in my name saying, 'I am He' and 'The time is at hand,' but do not follow them." The Catholic Church teaches us that instead of engaging in the useless task of trying to predict the time, dreading some awful day, we need to live in readiness and to wait in joyful hope for the coming of our Savior. What will that day be like? St. Paul writes, "Eye has not seen, ear has not heard, nor has it even dawned on human beings, the great things God has in store for those who love him."

Our second reading gives us some wonderful advice about how to live as we "wait in joyful hope" for the "wonderful things that God has in store for those who love him." First of all, it tell us to "rejoice always." This certainly does not mean going around grinning like a Cheshire cat all the time. It means that we remember in our heart of hearts, even on days when everything seems to be a total disaster, that we are destined to enjoy eternal happiness with God someday. It means, that in words of an old Quaker hymn, "through all the tumult and the strife, we hear the music ringing." It means to see the "image of God" in ourselves and others, no matter how much it may be overshadowed by our weaknesses, shortcomings and failures. It means to remember that there is a basic goodness in each and every person that cannot be lost or taken away. It means to celebrate our destiny as "children of God" and "heirs to the kingdom." Our reason to "rejoice always" does not come from our own successes or lack of them, but from God's unconditional love for us, in spite of what we have done or failed to do. Yes, we have reason to "rejoice always."

Second of all, it tells us to "pray unceasingly" while we wait. Again, this does not mean that we should all become obnoxious religious fanatics, turn our houses into churches, or try to live the lives of Trappist monks! It does mean that we should live in constant dialogue with God, seeking his advice and guidance on a daily basis. My own favorite way to pray is not saying formal prayers, even though I also do that. My favorite way to pray is to make myself aware of God's presence many times a day and to have a running conversation with God as I go about the routine of any given day. My favorite image of God is "companion," one who walks with me and talks to me and encourages me as I do the very ordinary things I have to do every day. No, I don't say formal prayers unceasingly, but I am in constant dialogue with God. Therefore I pray unceasingly.

Third, our second reading tells us to "give thanks constantly." Are you basically a thankful person? Do you realize just how blessed you are? Are you aware of the sacrifice that has been paid for your freedom? Are you aware of the number of friends and family members who love you? Do you realize just how privileged you are to live in this country, during these times: to have access to an education, an array of food, health care, a home? "Giving thanks constantly" is the opposite of taking things for granted and always whining about what's missing. "Giving thanks constantly" is impossible for people who believe that they are blessed because they deserve it or because they have earned it. In reality, everything we have, including the next breath we take, is a gift. Should we then not "give thanks constantly?"

In a couple of weeks, we will celebrate two thousand years since the coming of Jesus Christ into our world at that first Christmas, as well as two thousand years of waiting for his return. Since we "know not the day or the hour," we are invited to live lives of readiness, with our "belts fastened around our waists" and "our lamps burning ready." We wait, not in dread, but in joyful hope for the wonderful things that "eye has not seen, ear has not heard." How do we wait? Rejoicing always, praying unceasingly, and giving thanks constantly!

RECKONING

Lord, when did we see you hungry and feed you, or thirsty and give you drink; a stranger and welcome you, ill or in prison and visit you?

                                                 Matthew 25:44

My nephew, John, lives down in the country, and recently he told me about his speech to the FFA at Meade County High School on the care and feeding of sheep. I pointed out to him that he had never been around sheep in his life and, in fact, doesn't even live on a farm! It seems that he was pressured into filling in for someone else at the last minute. His whole speech was based on a few facts he had gleaned from reading a couple of pamphlets.

Most of us in modern day America have the same problem when it comes to many of the first century, middle eastern images we have in Scripture. It's harder for us to "get the point" since most of the time we have no personal experience of the images that Jesus used in his teaching. For example, probably most of us sitting in this room have never actually seen a live sheep, much less know anything about their habits and behaviors. The same can be said for goats!

To teach about the end of the world when all of us will stand before God for judgement, Jesus uses the image of a shepherd separating his sheep and goats at the end of the day. To help us "get the point," of what Jesus is trying to tell us, I have done a little research about this "sorting out" that shepherds did routinely in the time of Jesus.

People in those days very often had mixed herds of sheep and goats. Even though they were pastured together, they were very different from each other. That's why they had to be separated at night. Sheep, having dense wool coats, like to sleep out in the open. Goats, on the other hand, need shelter at night to keep warm. Sheep tend to suffer in silence, something that was admired by the ancients. Suffering in silence was considered to be a sign of a real man. So gradually over time, sheep came to symbolize honor, virility, and strength. That's why the sheep are the heroes in Jesus' story today. Goats, on the other hand, were associated with the devil. Unlike rams (male sheep), male goats allow other males access to their females. A goat doesn't care what goat is having sex with whom. A man whose wife was sleeping around was called a "goat." That's true even today in the middle east. Once a year, the Jews of Jesus' time ceremonially wrote out their sins and pinned them to a goat, then turned the goat loose in the desert. That's where we get the word"scapegoat," as in pinning the blame onto someone else. Goats, then, became a symbol of shame and shameful behavior. That's why they are the villains of Jesus' story today.

That is the background, but what does it mean? Jesus is talking again about the accounting that all of us will someday be required to give for the way we spent our lives. Just last week, Jesus told us that each one of us has been gifted and talented by God and that we will have to account for how we use what we have been given. The week before that,

Jesus talked about the wise and foolish virgins and how we must we live in readiness to meet God at anytime. Matthew's gospel is big on this idea of sifting, sorting, separating, and judgement: wheat versus chaff, the fruitful tree versus the barren one, the house built on rock versus the one built on sand, wheat versus weeds, good fish versus inedible trash fish, those with wedding garments versus those without.

If you have been following the readings along this last year, it should be clear by now that Jesus taught that there will **indeed** be a time for weeding out, sifting, separating, and sorting; a time when we will have to account for how we lived our lives here on earth! On this very last Sunday of the church year, we are given the criteria for judgement. Let's not get hung up too literally on the examples Jesus uses here, but let's look at the truth behind the examples. The criteria for God's time of weeding out, sifting, separating, and sorting is not just counting up your corporal works of mercy mentioned here (feeding the hungry, giving drink to the thirsty, welcoming strangers, clothing the naked, and visiting prisoners), but includes whether you were turned out or turned in, whether you saw yourself as a life-giver or life-taker, whether you were self-centered or other-centered, whether you saw yourself as a contributor to the human community or whether you saw the human community as here to serve you. Feeding the hungry, giving drink to the thirsty, welcoming strangers, clothing the naked, and visiting prisoners are only examples of actions that flow from a good heart.

These criteria are not new. They are a constant theme in sacred scripture from the beginning. When Cain asked, "Am

I my brother's keeper?" the answer came back, "Yes, you most certainly are!" Hospitality to strangers was one of the most sacred and fundamental duties of the Jewish faithful. Jesus said we are to love everyone, people of other religions, races, countries — **even** our enemies! The greatest commandment is to love our neighbors as ourselves. Dives' sin was not that he was rich, but that he didn't even see poor Lazarus, covered in sores and licked by dogs, sitting by his driveway every day! The whole point of Jesus coming in the flesh was to show us that when we serve others, we serve God himself. St. John says that if we say we love God and ignore the needs of the hurting and suffering people around us, we are liars!

The message these last few Sundays is very clear; there will be a time to give an accounting for the great gift of life; and the criteria for judgment is whether we were self-centered or other centered, tuned-in or turned off, selfish or generous, aware of others or oblivious to others, whether we gave to life or simply took from it, whether we understood that we were sent to serve the needs of the world or believed that the world was here to serve us! Those of us who think that we can make the cut simply by avoiding evil deeds are in for a rude awakening. The real test may come down to the good we failed to do! "As long as you failed to do it to one of these least ones, you failed to do it for me!" Over the years, I have heard a lot of confessions. People who do terrible things, are sorry, and want forgiveness, even seven times seventy times, don't bother me. The ones who irritate me are the people who come into confession and say, "Bless me, Father, I don't know what to tell you. I haven't done anything wrong. I haven't stolen. I haven't committed adultery. I haven't cheated anybody. I haven't lied." So often, I have wanted to pull the curtain back and yell, "Well, goody for you! You are now at zero! Now, when are you going to start living the Christian life? What good have you done?" The Christian life is about a lot more than avoiding evil! It is about actively doing good, for Christ's sake!!! The old *Confiteor*, a prayer we used to say when the Mass was in Latin, empasized this: "I confess . . . that I have sinned . . . in what I have done **and** what I have failed to do!"

"Lord, when did we see you hungry or thirsty or a stranger or naked or sick or in prison and did not take care of you?" God will answer, "What you did not do for one of these least ones, you did not do for me."